Rescuing
the
21st
Century
Marriage

Rescuing the 21st Century Marriage

by
Harold McDougal

(with a final chapter by Diane McDougal)

Destiny Image Publishers
P.O. Box 351
Shippensburg, PA 17257

ISBN 1-56043-059-1

Printed in the U.S.A.
For Worldwide Distribution

Other books by Harold McDougal:

Principles of Christian Faith, Volume I

The Master Keys Series:
  Speaking in Tongues
  Who Are We in Christ?
  Secrets of Success

Order from:

World Missions
P.O. Box 404
Williamsport, MD 21795

To Diane, my bride of 25 years.

Entreat me not to leave thee, or to return from following after thee: for whither thou goest, I will go; and where thou lodgest, I will lodge: thy people shall be my people, and thy God my God:

Where thou diest, will I die, and there will I be buried: the Lord do so to me, and more also, if ought but death part thee and me.

Ruth 1:16-17

Acknowledgements

One of my duties during the past few years has been in the editing and rewriting of Christian materials for publication. Because of that I think I appreciate more than most the delicacy of criticism. An editor is sometimes unsure of just how far to go with the criticism of a manuscript. A lot depends on how well we know the author and how well they know us. The confidence developed in close friendship frees us from some of the natural restraints of constructive criticism.

As always I am deeply indebted to the good number of close friends and family members who reviewed this manuscript over the past months and gave me their valuable suggestions for its improvement. Thank you!

Contents

Introduction

The devastating influences that attack marriage these days have no respect of persons. This modern-day scourge affects not only Hollywood stars, rock performers, politicians and wealthy business people. Now, it strikes born-again Christians. It strikes ministers. It strikes missionaries.

There is no single answer for every case of failing or broken marriage. The subject is complex because human nature is complex, and because we are living in a complex and troubled society. I am not married to the person you are married to. The person you are married to may not be the person you thought you married a few years ago.

I don't want to trivialize or seem to have pat answers. There are none. There are, however, certain

Biblical principles that I feel are basic to every situation. And one thing is certain, only God can resolve many marital disputes and return harmony and peace to the home.

Will these principles work in your case? It certainly can't hurt to try.

The comment of one of my close friends who did me the favor of reviewing the manuscript for *Rescuing the 21st Century Marriage* was, "You seem to be so aloof from the subject throughout." I knew exactly what he meant.

During the preparation of the manuscript I had to make a hard decision about the inclusion of personal experience. Believe me, we are not aloof from this material. We experienced it. We went through our own private hell. We are writing from our hearts. At one point I wrote large sections of material on our own experience. After I had prayed about it though, I eventually decided not to include it for several reasons:

Our experience is unique in many ways. We left for the mission field soon after we were married. Our marriage was complicated by our living in a foreign country (far from family and friends), of working under national church groups (without the normal moral and financial support that missionaries depend on), by the raising of our family under extreme circumstances, etc. I felt that most people would think that our experience was so different from their own that these teachings were not applicable to real life. I am sure, however, that the underlying struggle we experienced in our marriage is identical to that which others face.

Secondly, I thought that the tales of our experiences — so romantic and exciting to most people who have never had the privilege of spending years among the diverse peoples of the third world countries — could very easily overshadow the theme of the book and become the principle object of attention. And finally, as public people it is not convenient for us to relate our experience in detail. Suffice it to say that our marriage was all but destroyed, yet the principles that we put forth in the following pages not only rescued it from that almost certain destruction, but gave us a happiness together normally reserved for fairy tales.

We believe what we are telling you.

Chapter 1

Decide Your Marriage is Worth Rescuing

The first step in rescuing your marriage is to decide you want to do it. That is half the battle.

If students have no desire to learn, no motivation to excel, no reason to exert themselves, they simply don't. Any worthy goal in life takes discipline and effort. Those who want to learn to ski badly enough, for instance, do whatever is necessary.

Olympic stars have a driving desire to win, most often instilled in them by their parents. If they don't have it, they never get that far.

Mending a damaged marriage requires some hard decisions, some sacrifice, some effort, some patience. It is much easier to just say, "It's not worth it," and give up. Most people divorce because they tire of the struggle. More and more, divorce is being touted by "experts" as the easy solution.

"The spark is gone."

"There is no love left."

"Every exchange is a bitter one."

"Why prolong the agony?"

"Wouldn't it be better for everyone involved just to end it now?"

If you can get over this first hurdle, you are on your way to victory. You cannot save your marriage if you don't want to save it. And why should you work toward saving your marriage? What could motivate you to do that? We need motivation for most anything that we do. If there is a large amount of money involved in some endeavor, look for many people to get involved. Money is a great "motivator." If there exists the possibility of fame, expect many participants. The possibility of becoming famous is a great "motivator." We need motivation.

A well used slogan of our day is, "What's in it for me?" That is not an entirely unchristian concept. The Bible teaches us to avoid things that are not for our good and do things which are. There are two very great differences in the Christian application of this truth. One, we trust God to decide what is good for us and what is not. Secondly, we trust His Word when He tells us something is good for us — even when we can't see how it could be.

So, why save your marriage? Let me give you the reasons I believe your marriage is worth saving. All of them may not apply to your situation, but don't reject those that do.

Reasons for wanting to save your marriage:

The Sense of Failure

Who likes to fail? Failing at anything leaves deep psychological scars. Some people never get over failing classes, failing to make the team, failing to get the job, etc. Failure can be devastating. Those whose marriages fail often go through life with a defeatist attitude. "I am a failure." "I can't do anything right."

Having failed in marriage affects many people's attitude about their work, their ongoing education, their other relationships, etc. They often need extensive psychological counseling and sometimes never recover.

The Wasted Years

Marriage is hard work. You spend years developing a relationship, developing trust, developing an understanding, developing a life together. What a waste to throw that all away! Who will share those memories with you now? Who will appreciate what you have been doing these many years? Don't throw it to the wind! Meaningful relationships are beyond monetary value. They are priceless. None of them is perfect. Make the best of them.

Young people are up in arms about the way we are damaging the ecology, our oceans, our skies, etc. What about the psychological pollution of our world — failure and waste. These are devastating losses for future generations, and everyone on our planet will be affected.

Who knows you better than your spouse? How many years would it take to develop a similar relationship with another person? Is it even possible? Can the same level of intimacy ever be developed with a new mate? Don't take the risk.

For the Children's Sake

For centuries men and women stayed in bad marriages "for the children's sake." Now, that reasoning has been thrown aside and a new reasoning developed: "What could be worse for the children than to live in that poisoned atmosphere?" Believe me, there could be worse things:

* Being party to the bitter child-custody battles

* Being used by either or both parents to "get back at" the other

* Being shunted from house to house in a game of wills

* Suffering the permanent loss of one parent (worse, according to psychologists, than losing a parent by death)

* Suffering the embarrassment (among their friends and classmates) associated with divorce

The worst thing perhaps is that children blame themselves for their parents' difficulties. "If I had only been better, done better, this wouldn't have happened."

Children often begin to hate one or the other of their parents or both:

"Why did he/she submit me to this humiliation?"
"Why did he/she abandon me?"
"He/she doesn't love me."

Children are not capable of handling all this psychological baggage. It is bound to take its toll on them sooner or later. Recent studies show that a great number of children who fail in school, who start taking drugs, and who become promiscuous at an early age, are simply reacting to the hurts of divorce and its terrible aftermath.

Children are often devastated when a parent begins to date other people. "How could they?"

Children are often the losers in a second marriage. Who can love them like their own father or mother?

In the end, most of what a parent tries to do for his or her own happiness affects adversely the children. Can the result be satisfying? Is some imagined personal pleasure worth the psychological destruction of the children? Maybe a selfish, uncaring and willful parent could answer "yes." A Christian may not.

Many studies show that children are the ones who suffer most economically from divorce. I will elaborate on that later.

Divorce Complicates Your Life

When most people divorce, they are seeking to put an end to misunderstandings, put the past in the past, and get on with life. Boy, do they have a rude shock coming! Divorce complicates your life in every way.

We think we don't have enough time now. When we have to juggle schedules with parents living in two different houses (perhaps in two different towns), life really gets complicated.

If you thought it was difficult to keep up with children's clothes, wait until they need clothes in two houses. They will never be where they need them when they need them. Which parent is responsible for keeping the clothes clean? Each will expect the other to be responsible and will have no way of knowing whether the other has remembered or not.

And that is just the beginning. Consider school activities in which parents are invited to participate: PTA, open house, parent's night, award banquets, graduation, etc. Consider birthdays, Christmas, Thanksgiving etc. These wonderful holidays should be looked forward to as special occasions in which we should be able to express our love to each other and enjoy each other's company. Instead, divorced couples dread the approach of these days. They are tense times of juggling schedules in order to do the right thing and still avoid ugly confrontations. Nobody wins. Everybody loses.

Divorce is Expensive — in Every Way

We seldom think of divorce as an economic problem.

It is. In fact, it is one of the greatest causes of poverty in America. It is difficult enough to keep one home and one set of children. When confronted with alimony, child support, the need for a second home, a second car, more clothes, and extra travel expenses, many families are devastated and never recover economically. Everyone loses, but the children lose most.

Second Marriage Failures

Divorced people have many strikes against them. They have heavy psychological burdens and heavy financial burdens. Their life has become so complicated, so stressful. They are torn in several directions. All of this puts strain on second marriages. Failures in second marriages are even higher than in first marriages.

The second failure fortifies the psychological and financial problems, leaving many people totally devastated and unable to continue functioning as normal human beings. They become cynical, distrustful, and resentful. They are just ticking time bombs, waiting to explode.

What guarantees do you have in a second marriage? You can fall out of love with the second mate just as you did with the first. You can have a communications breakdown with the second just as with the first. You can have differences over money with the second just as with the first.

The dangers the second marriage presents lead many people to live as swinging singles. Believe me, that is no solution. You may think you are having a ball now, but down the road you will be forced to count the cost. You can't afford it!

Nothing is Resolved

Nothing is resolved by divorce. You are simply running from the problem. Do we quit when studies get too demanding? Do we give up when problems confront us in business? Do we give up when we are behind in a sports event? Giving up on your marriage without resolving anything may lead you to give up on life in general. It is a dangerous precedent. You may never recover.

Nothing is resolved in the relationship with your ex-spouse. If children are involved, you still have to maintain some semblance of relationship for their sake. How do you know, for instance, what time to pick them up (from the other house) or what time they will be picked up (at your house).

Although these reasons for saving your marriage are compelling, there are other, more important reasons. I have left the most important reasons until last — so that I wouldn't sound preachy:

God's Will

A believer's first consideration is always God's will. A believer wants to please God and knows that pleasing God is wise. His will is always best for us. He has this to say about marriage:

*Have ye not read, that he which made them at the
beginning made them male and female,
And said, For this cause shall a man leave father and
mother, and shall cleave to his wife: and they twain
shall be one flesh?
Wherefore they are no more twain, but one flesh.
What therefore God hath joined together, let not man
put asunder.*

Matthew 19:4-6

God knows that breaking the mystical bond created in
marriage leaves deep psychological scars. He knows
that failure in marriage leaves many with a deep sense
of personal failure. He knows that divorce complicates
your life not only psychologically, but financially and
physically. He knows that failing in marriage leaves a
sense of guilt that is extremely difficult to overcome. He
knows that all your future relationships in both your
professional and social life will be adversely affected. He
knows that your children may never recover. Why don't
we trust Him? He knows what is best for us! Believe
Him!

For The Good of Your Soul

The loss of a mate through divorce or separation
creates a worse trauma, according to experts in the field,
than their loss through death. The resulting sense of
frustration, bitterness, guilt, and loneliness often does
the soul great harm. Perhaps most dangerous of all,
divorce sets you up psychologically for a worse mistake.

You become vulnerable. You are not thinking clearly. In practice it is called "on the rebound." You may do things you know are unwise. Why put yourself in that position? Why put your soul at risk? Why complicate life?

Your Testimony to the Community

As believers, we realize that what we do affects everyone around us. Smokers are recently learning that what they do is not just their own business. Second-hand smoke is proving more deadly than smoking itself.

At the same time, society is trying to convince us that what we do is our own business. We needn't think about anyone else when we make a decision. "If it feels good, do it." We know that philosophy is not Christian. Our testimony in the community is of utmost importance. God's Word tells us:

> *Only let your conversation* [manner of living] *be as it becometh the gospel of Christ: that whether I come and see you, or else be absent, I may hear of your affairs, that ye stand fast in one spirit, with one mind striving together for the faith of the gospel.*
> Philippians 1:27

Aspiring to the Ministry

Those who have a desire for ministry must realize that, in the last decade of the twentieth century, divorce is still a blight on any record. Given the sheer numbers of divorced people in our country, many churches have been forced to adjust their expectations. Still, nobody is happy to know that you have been divorced. It places a series of question marks in everyone's mind about your person, about your ability to help others, about your suitability for public ministry, about your suitability for leadership roles.

When Paul gave Timothy guidelines concerning the type of person to select for office in the Church, he suggested that he look for those who knew how to get their own house in order (1 Timothy 3:1-13). That guideline was divinely inspired and became part of the Word of God for all succeeding generations.

Throwing your marriage away may mark you to be passed over when decisions are made for future ministry.

Make a conscious decision that you want to save your marriage. You have every reason to do so.

Chapter 2

Get Your Thinking Straightened Out

The second step to saving your marriage is a whole new way of thinking about the institution of marriage itself. So much of our thinking these days is formed by public opinion, by advertising campaigns, by the concepts of popular politicians and well-known television personalities. What happened to God? Have we asked His opinion recently?

Daily we are bombarded by the thoughts of this expert and that expert until we become confused as to what part of our thinking is Christian and which part is secular. It is astonishing to think that many of the pet phrases which have made their way into the work place of

America and into our thinking as individuals have their roots in the pagan Oriental religions. This twisting of our thinking is a major contributor to the divorce epidemic. Society has no respect now for God's thoughts.

Most people know that divorce is not God's will. But, other thoughts crowd in upon that one and override it until divorce seems like the perfect solution, not the door to greater problems.

We are confused. We need to get our thinking straightened out. We have believed too much of the media hype. We have read too many magazines, listened to too many experts on television talk shows. We need to give God a chance to talk to us about His design for marriage.

Some people go about things backwards. Instead of taking the positive reasons to save their marriage, they need to look at everything from the opposite end. They need to see the fallacy of all the pat reasons commonly given for dissolving a marriage. They need to get their thinking straightened out.

"I don't love him/her anymore!"

This certainly is a serious problem. The feeling of love is very important in the marriage. It is one of the glues that holds everything together. When the glue begins to lose its power, everything begins to go wrong.

As believers, what we need to remember is that what the world calls "love" is not true love. God is love. Love is of God. God is the Author of love. Lost love is not a serious problem to the Author of love. Lost love can be regained. Any new love that might seem exciting to us can fail and often does. Any new flame may dim. That lost feeling of love in the present marriage can be regained. That flame can be rekindled. And rekindled love is ardent.

Perhaps you don't have the feeling of love for him/her anymore. Misunderstandings, hurts, and frustrations are all enemies of the love feeling. Remove the misunderstandings and the embers of love can burst forth into renewed flame. Heal the hurts and the feelings can emerge stronger than ever.

"There is too much bitterness here!
I don't think it can be resolved!"

Bitterness is a terrible thing. It gets down into a person's spirit and affects everything about their personality. It is ironic that bitterness develops in marriage. Marriage is intended to be the most satisfying of human relationships. The most intimate experiences are reserved for marriage. But, that is exactly what makes marriage so vulnerable to damage.

Since marriage is the most intimate human relationship, what happens there affects you more deeply than anything else in life. The joys of marriage cannot be compared with success in the office. In the same way, the hurts that result in marriage are more devastating to you than anything you can experience in any other area of life. They hit you in the deepest part of your being. The result is often a deep bitterness. The sweetest thing in your life has become the most bitter thing in your life.

That problem should not be minimized. But, bitterness can be healed. The roots of the problem can be dealt with.

And if you think there is bitterness now, just imagine the bitterness produced by a heated child-custody battle, alimony battle and child-support battle. Nothing compares with it in the legal world. As the saying goes, "You ain't seen nothing yet!"

If bitterness is your problem, why invite more bitterness? Nip bitterness in the bud! Go to the root of the problem! Let God heal the hurts and resolve the issues. Nothing is too hard for the Lord!

"He/she doesn't understand me!"

Marital conflicts complicate our conversations so much that we misinterpret what the other is saying. We read into their words things that were not intended and miss entirely the true intent. Both are hurt — the hearer, for what is imagined, and the speaker, because he/she is misunderstood.

"He/she doesn't understand me" is a legitimate complaint. But, if your spouse doesn't understand you, who can? Misunderstandings have been part of the human relationship from the beginning of time. They have been the cause of wars, of racial prejudice.

When we get to know people, when we understand better their thinking processes, when we understand what motivates them to say certain things and do certain things, we often overlook what they say and justify them to others. "He didn't mean that like it sounded. He's been under a lot of stress lately."

But when we are hurt, we subconsciously want to read the wrong thing into the words of others. We want to imagine the worst of their intentions. A vicious cycle of thrust and counter-thrust develops.

When you understand what is happening, it takes very little time to heal these differences. The most terrible arguments of married couples often end in the most passionate embraces. Believe for it!

No one has the potential to understand you better than your mate, but your mate is human, is under a lot of stress, is not thinking clearly. Help your mate to understand you. Don't write off the marriage because of misunderstood conversation.

I know several couples who married without being able to speak the language of the other very well. You think you have problems! Explain to me why they are still together after so many years.

"We're so different!"

One of the age-old controversies among marriage counselors and psychologists concerns whether or not it is important to be alike, enjoy the same things, have the same goals in life.

I have always been fascinated by the custom of many families in India. The parents place announcements in the newspaper, advertising for a mate for their son or daughter. Because they are looking for a person of a similar age, with the same educational level, the same social status, the same goals in life, they list their child's "qualifications." Or, they may specify exactly what they are looking for in a mate for their offspring.

The marriage is arranged by the parents, and the young couple sometimes barely knows each other before the marriage is consummated. They have little say in the matter. Even so, they swear that it works wonderfully. They learn to love each other because they are similar in so many ways.

We have to admit that we enjoy being around people who have the same interests. We like to talk to people who understand what we are talking about. There is a certain security in the known and recognizable. This fact often leads to extramarital affairs among people who work together and share interests in some way. The rationale is that this person understands us better than our mate.

On the other hand, it is a proven fact that opposites attract. Even in nature, males and females are not alike. The differences are remarkable for their purpose. The males are perfect for their role and the females for theirs. They balance each other.

I believe it is the same with us humans. I have seen it happen time and time again. We are attracted to people with whom we have little in common. The difference is what attracts us. After we are married, the very thing that attracted us to each other begins to repel us. "Why is he/she so different?" "Do we have anything in common?" Not much.

We have different tastes in food. We have different tastes in clothes. We have different tastes in furniture. We have different tastes in perfume. We have different tastes in friends. We have different hobbies. We have different goals. This fact creates enormous potential for conflict. Yet, we must recognize that many differences which exist between spouses are for our own good. For example:

Diane	Harold
Is outgoing	Is introvertish
Is warm-blooded	Is cold-blooded
Falls asleep easily	Must read to fall asleep
Is an early riser	Is a later riser
Is inspirational	Is methodical
Loves acrobatics	Isn't crazy about acrobatics
Isn't crazy about music	Loves music
Isn't crazy about horseback riding	Loves to ride horses
Loves to play tennis	Isn't crazy about tennis
Likes Dove soap	Prefers Irish Spring
Likes Crest toothpaste	Prefers Colgate
Likes a style of interior decorating known as "controlled clutter."	Wants his surroundings to be orderly
Drinks coffee	Prefers tea
Makes friends easily	Doesn't make friends easily
Always wants desert	Rarely wants desert
Enjoys social functions	Doesn't enjoy social functions

There is only one biblical rule on how we must be alike: God's Word admonishes us not to marry an unbeliever (2 Corinthians 6:14). We have also discovered through the years that those who are interested in the ministry should marry someone with a similar interest. Beyond that, it is not necessary for us to be alike in every way.

It is the lack of tolerance for differences in taste, style, thought, etc. that has caused racial and religious prejudices in so many parts of the world. Yet, in the days in which we are living, many people are learning not to despise someone else just because the color of the skin is different, because they eat something different or have different customs. There are some classic examples:

Many people think the Latins must be beasts to allow someone to torment a poor bull and cheer when it is mortally wounded. The Latins cannot understand how we Americans can let men on a football field jump on top of each other and hurt each other. Their "futbal," (soccer) is so much more civilized.

Americans who visit India wonder why the Indians take a bath from a bucket, gradually pouring water over themselves with a dipper. Indians wonder why Americans get in a tub, wash off in the water and then sit in that dirty water.

The point is that people are very different and can easily misunderstand one another. When we discover why they are different and why they like certain things, we understand them and even appreciate them. Don't write people off simply because they are different.

People who live together long enough learn from each other and develop many of the same tastes. They never develop all the same tastes, however. They always remain different.

If people of diverse races and creeds can learn to live together in peace in the world, can't we learn to live with a person who is different in the marriage? The differences in marriage are for our benefit. They are for balance. Meticulously neat people often marry those who are less than neat. Methodical people often marry those who do things only by inspiration. Quiet people often marry those who are talkative. Quiet people can be drawn out by a talkative mate, and talkative people can learn to be good listeners, as well.

If you always remember that the purpose of attracting the opposite type is for balance, life will be a lot easier for you. Learn to appreciate the differences rather than despise them.

Who doesn't marvel at nature. It is still amazing to the greatest of scientists: the intricacy of a tiny flower, of a rain drop, of a snow flake, of an insect's eye, of the human body, let alone the vast reaches of space and its untapped mysteries. What a marvel our God has created!

He knows what He is doing. Electricity lights our homes because it was discovered that using a positive charge and a negative ground, so opposed that they make sparks when they touch, produces electrical energy. Neither the positive nor the negative are useful alone. Both are needed.

Magnets which have the same poles facing each other repel each other. Opposites attract. God designed all that. He designed the balance of nature.

Being different is not all bad. It has its purposes. Men and women are totally different creatures — not only physically, but psychologically. They are millions of miles apart. Yet, they attract each other and sometimes the most different ones attract each other the most.

God knows what He is doing. He made things attract

each other for a purpose. He puts them together for balance. How boring it would be if we always knew what the other was thinking, always anticipated every action. Variety is the spice of life. Don't knock it. God has placed in the Body of Christ diverse gifts, diverse ministries and diverse manifestations of those gifts and ministries. He doesn't make us all alike. *"If the whole body were an eye,"* He tells us, *"where were the hearing?"* (1 Corinthians 12:17).

Stop expecting everybody to think exactly like you. Stop expecting everyone to always agree with you. Stop expecting everyone to like the same things you like and want the same things you want. Broaden your scope. Enlarge your sights. Make an effort to understand your mate. The things they do which drive you absolutely crazy may be God-given balances in your marriage.

"It was a mistake from the start!"

Maybe! Maybe it was a mistake from the start! But, maybe it wasn't! In the heat of marital disputes we often jump to wrong conclusions. Our reasoning ability is affected. We are not thinking clearly. We probably need the intervention of a third person to help us remember, to think clearly, to weigh everything.

Even if it was a mistake from the start, can another mistake correct it? We are prone to make mistakes when our emotions have run away from us and we are not thinking clearly. Just as many mistakes are made in the heat of passionate rejection as are made in the heat of passionate acceptance. Be careful. A second mistake doesn't make the first one right.

God judges us by our actions today. He has already

forgotten yesterday. We should too. Whatever mistakes we may have made in the past should not affect our present decision. In God the past is buried and forgotten. Don't use the past as the basis for a major decision. Our decisions are based on God's will today.

The Bible makes it clear that divorce is acceptable only in the most extreme cases. Even then it is not God's best. It will not solve anything and will complicate your life. Believe God's Word. Decide that you want to save your marriage.

"He/she doesn't make me happy!"

God wants you to be happy. But, the idea that marriage can make you happy is a mistaken one. Marriage was never meant by God to meet all our emotional needs. In fact nothing in this world is designed to satisfy all our emotional needs.

The physical aspect of the marriage relationship can be likened to our other appetites. We eat (and we do eat some wonderful things) and after a little while we are hungry again. We are looking for something that will "hit the spot." We rarely find it. When we do it is very temporary. Food was not meant to totally satisfy us.

Food does, however, serve a healthy purpose for us and for that reason we are attracted to it. Our body needs the nourishment it provides. It gives us strength, causes us to grow.

We drink something, and in no time at all, we are thirsty again. What we are drinking is soothing, delicious, even healthful, but it satisfies for only a short time.

It was not meant to bring lasting satisfaction. We have a built-in mechanism called "thirst" that makes us want to drink because our body needs the liquid it derives from the drink.

The physical aspect of marriage serves a very healthy and good purpose. But it was never meant to totally satisfy our needs. It has been highly overrated.

Human companionship cannot totally satisfy our emotional need. The most contented individuals have fellowship with God, fellowship with the church, fellowship with the family and fellowship with a spouse. It takes all these elements — working together — to bring about the desired happiness. One person cannot possibly meet all our emotional needs.

Even at that, our happiness is not complete. We are living as strangers and pilgrims on this earth. We will never be totally happy until we are in the presence of the Lord. We were not meant to be satisfied by an earthly relationship.

The famous hymnwriter, Fanny J. Crosby, had a great revelation:

> *There are depths of love that I may not know*
> *Till I cross the narrow sea*
> *There are heights of joy that I may not reach*
> *Till I rest in peace with Thee*

The world paints a false picture in movies, books, and advertisements of a peace and joy that are actually inaccessible here on this earth. Here we will have only a foretaste of Heaven. Many more joys will be reserved for us there.

Martin Luther was so happily married that he felt every man should die in the arms of his wife. He advised his fellow ministers that the best possible place they could be found at the second coming of the Lord would be in ardent embrace with their wives. Martin Luther had many other good things going for him, however. He was rediscovering the great Christian principles and leading the Church out of the dark ages. The joy he felt could not have been found only in the arms of a wife. God reserves for Himself the greatest joys and the greatest relationship of love.

Get your thinking straightened out.

Chapter 3

Take Full Responsibility For the Past

The next step you must take to save your marriage is to accept full responsibility for the past. Someone has to do it, and you are probably more to blame than you know or care to admit. By accepting full responsibility you do several things. First, you show your desire to save the marriage. Your mate doesn't believe you care. This action shows that you do.

Secondly, you get the ball rolling – whether there is a positive reaction from your spouse or not. And, since you are willing to accept full responsibility, you are not devastated if your mate accepts no responsibility at all.

Thirdly, you are obeying God, for His Word teaches you to do it, as we shall see.

Some of us are such idealists. To us there exists only right and wrong, black and white, in or out. "If I am right, I am right." What we have to learn is that while we are sure we are right, we are often wrong. The Bible says, *"When you think you are standing, be careful, because you may be about to fall"* (1 Corinthians 10:12/Paraphrased).

You have been wrong and done wrong. You may not think so, but I guarantee it. Because of our differences, we often offend other people unknowingly. In the marriage these offenses are magnified. You may forget the circumstance in which the other person is offended. It means nothing to you. Your mate, however, doesn't forget it and can repeat back to you every word spoken at that moment, can describe in detail every action taken.

One Sunday morning, while we were living in Ecuador, I was answering the question of a Colombian Sister after the morning Church service. While we were talking, someone called me from the balcony to say something. I turned to hear the short message and then resumed the conversation.

Some weeks later the pastor and I decided to visit the Colombian couple, because they had not been attending the church regularly. When we asked why they had not been coming, I was shocked to hear her say, "Because of the way you insulted me."

I was incredulous. "What did I do to offend you? Please tell me. I was unaware that I had done anything."

She remembered the exact words we had been saying, who it was that called to me, what exactly they said, and most of all (against Latin custom), that I had failed to ask her to please excuse me for a moment and to wait for her consent before I turned away and broke the flow of conversation.

There are so many customs like that which we can unknowingly break that I got in the habit of saying anywhere I went, "Friends, Brothers and Sisters, I am new to your culture and I have much to learn about proper etiquette. Please make me aware of it. I want to learn."

Then when I was leaving anywhere, I learned to say in the customary farewell address, "If I have unknowingly done anything to offend anyone while I have been here, I ask you to be forgiving. I love you, although I am a 'gringo.' " The effect was powerful. When you are willing to admit that you offend, people are not offended.

Exactly the same thing happens within the context of the marriage. We think we know each other. We think we understand each other. Yet, we interpret words and actions very differently than they were intended. *We unknowingly offend.* We are busy with our own thoughts and plans sometimes and are insensitive to the needs and desires of our mate. We unknowingly offend. We spend so much of our time trying to figure out what the other person is thinking, what we have done wrong. When we recognize the dangers of mis-communication, we can be more careful to make ourselves understood.

During marital disputes, if we ask one or both of the partners to jot down the things that offend them, each one can come up with a very long list. They can remember hurts everyone thought were long since buried and forgotten. Everything gets dug up at this point and rehashed. This is the opposite of what needs to be done.

If we enter into a round of recriminations and counter recriminations, this could go on forever. Every round heats the atmosphere up even more. As words fly freely back and forth, we get further and further from the goal. The scene will probably end in a tragic brawl that everyone will later be sorry for, but the damage will have been done.

There is but one solution. You must do as Jesus did. He didn't come to condemn. He didn't come to point the finger. He didn't come to put man in his place. He came with a forgiving spirit. He prayed, *"Father, forgive them. For they know not what they do"* (Luke 23:34). That prayer helped me to love drunkards and murderers and prostitutes and drug addicts. Can't we love and forgive our own spouses?

By taking responsibility for the past you are showing forth a Christ-like spirit. He certainly was guiltless, yet He took blame upon Himself. You are not guiltless, and don't start feeling like some martyr. Start recognizing the truth — the truth about yourself.

You think you are the responsible person in this marriage, then start acting like it. You think you are right, then do the right thing. You think you know better, then do better.

In any position of leadership, a heavier burden falls upon those in greater responsibility. If misunderstandings arise, leaders must make an effort to face the person or persons involved and get to the bottom of the matter. The very best and fastest way to do that is to accept full blame for whatever has happened. "I think I must have offended you in some way. I notice that our relationship is not as good as before. Tell me about it."

That won't kill you, and chances are that you have done something that you are not aware of. If you haven't, if offenses are imagined, if they are a result of a misunderstanding, etc. what does it hurt to approach it in this manner? A big person can do it. Only little people insist on their innocence and demand that the other person come to them and ask forgiveness in order to start a dialogue.

You need to go further. Don't wait for your spouse to give you the list of offenses. Ask God to show you every time you have hurt your mate. Ask Him to show you every offensive conversation, every offensive action, everything you didn't do that you should have done, everything you didn't say that you should have said. Then, when you approach your mate, you have specifics.

For now, forget every petty complaint you have yourself. Concentrate on what you have done to contribute to the problem. You are responsible before God for your own deeds. The sins and failures of others will often correct themselves if you get yourself straightened out.

Jesus said it was dangerous to offend other people:

> *But whoso shall offend one of these little ones which*
> *believe in me, it were better for him that a millstone*
> *were hanged about his neck, and that he were*
> *drowned in the depth of the sea.*
>
> Matthew 18:6

God doesn't take it lightly when we offend His little
ones. When we offend them, we are offending God. The
quality of your relationship to God is being compro-
mised by your marital problems. You can't afford that.
You can't afford for your soul to suffer. You must act
quickly. The Word is clear:

When you have offended one of God's little ones, He
doesn't accept your gifts to Him.

> *Therefore if thou bring thy gift to the altar, and there*
> *rememberest that thy brother hath ought against thee;*
> *Leave there thy gift before the altar, and go thy way;*
> *first be reconciled to thy brother, and then come and*
> *offer thy gift.*   Matthew 5:23-24

When you have offended one of God's little ones, you
have no right to partake of the communion table. If you do
partake, you are eating and drinking "damnation" to
yourself.

> *For he that eateth and drinketh unworthily, eateth*
> *and drinketh damnation to himself, not discerning*

> *the Lord's body. For this cause many are weak and sickly among you, and many sleep.*
>
> 1 Corinthians 11:29-30

When you refuse to be reconciled to one of God's little ones, He refuses to hear your prayer for forgiveness.

> *And forgive us our debts, as we forgive our debtors. And lead us not into temptation, but deliver us from evil: For thine is the kingdom, and the power, and the glory, for ever. Amen.*
>
> *For if ye forgive men their trespasses, your heavenly Father will also forgive you: But if ye forgive not men their trespasses, neither will your Father forgive your trespasses.*
>
> Matthew 6:12-15

Lest you think that none of these passages relates to the marriage relationship, Peter directly addressed the issue:

> *Likewise, ye husbands, dwell with them according to knowledge, giving honour unto the wife, as unto the weaker vessel, and as being heirs together of the grace of life; that your prayers be not hindered.*
>
> 1 Peter 3:7

A bad marriage relationship will hinder your prayers and put your soul in danger. After exhorting Christian wives on ways to win their unsaved husbands to the Lord

(1 Peter 3:1-6), and exhorting husbands that a bad
marriage relationship will surely hinder their prayers
(verse 7), Peter continued with these words:

> *Finally, be ye all of one mind, having compassion one*
> *of another, love as brethren, be pitiful [tenderhearted],*
> *be courteous: Not rendering evil for evil, or railing*
> *for railing: but contrariwise blessing; knowing that*
> *ye are thereunto called, that ye should inherit a*
> *blessing.*
>
> *For he that will love life, and see good days, let him*
> *refrain his tongue from evil, and his lips that they*
> *speak no guile:*
> *Let him eschew evil, and do good; let him seek peace,*
> *and ensue it.*
> *For the eyes of the Lord are over the righteous, and*
> *his ears are open unto their prayers: but the face of*
> *the Lord is against them that do evil.*
>
> *And who is he that will harm you, if ye be followers*
> *of that which is good? But and if ye suffer for*
> *righteousness' sake, happy are ye: and be not afraid*
> *of their terror, neither be troubled; But sanctify the*
> *Lord God in your hearts: and be ready always to give*
> *an answer to every man that asketh you a reason of*
> *the hope that is in you with meekness and fear:*
> *Having a good conscience; that, whereas they speak*
> *evil of you, as of evildoers, they may be ashamed that*
> *falsely accuse your good conversation in Christ. For*
> *it is better, if the will of God be so, that ye suffer for*
> *well doing, than for evil doing.*

*For Christ also hath once suffered for sins, the just
for the unjust, that he might bring us to God, being
put to death in the flesh, but quickened by the spirit:*
1 Peter 3:8-18

Where did he stop talking about marriage and start
talking about the everyday Christian life? Most Bibles
that divide chapters into subjects make the logical division between verses 7 and 8. But is there a division
there? Can we rightly separate home life from the daily
Christian life? If we can't live the Christian life at home,
where can we live it?

God will not ignore your offense toward your husband
or wife. He/she is one of His little ones. If you offend one
of His little ones, He said, He cannot take it lightly.

He told us that if we feed *"one of the least of these My
brethren,"* we are actually feeding Him (Matthew 25:40).
If we clothe *"one of the least of these My brethren,"* we are
actually clothing Him. If we visit *"one of the least of these
my brethren,"* we are actually visiting Him. So, if we offend
"one of the least of these My brethren," we are actually
offending Him.

God loves His little ones. He cannot permit us to
offend them with impunity. If you offend one of His little
ones, it would be better for you to put a millstone around
your neck and cast yourself into the sea. If you offend
one of His little ones, the quality of your relationship
with God is affected, He cannot accept your offerings,
He cannot bless you in the communion, He cannot
forgive your sins, He cannot answer your prayer.

You cannot afford to live in bitterness and resent-
ment. Whatever your mate does, you must decide to
take full responsibility for the past. Peter ended this
third chapter with the paragraph beginning, *"For Christ
also hath once suffered for sins, the just for the unjust, that he
might bring us to God ... ."* You may well be what we
commonly call "the innocent party." You may well be
the more nearly correct of the two. You may be the more
spiritual. That is all the more reason that you should
take the responsibility. If you don't, who will?

You must. You cannot afford to do otherwise. The
welfare of your soul demands it. You must forgive
whatever hurts or imagined hurts you feel, while recognizing any and all wrongs you have committed against
your mate, God's little one.

If you take responsibility for the past, you can stop
spinning your wheels in endless recriminations and
start moving forward into healing. This is an essential
step. Don't try to sidestep it. God will not honor it. If you,
however, demonstrate His Spirit, He will work miracu-
lously for you and do for you what you cannot do for
yourself.

By "accepting responsibility for the past" I certainly
do not mean that you should feel condemned or even
blame yourself for the failures of your marriage. I mean
that nobody has to be blamed at all. Wipe the slate clean
and start over, without the necessity of leveling blame.
That is the Christ-like thing to do!

Chapter 4

Exercise Your Faith

As believers we have access to the power of God. We have resources available to us that others could only dream about. Thank God for His help. Unbelievers may do all the right things and yet come to no good conclusion. We can expect the miraculous intervention of our all powerful God. We must exercise our faith toward that goal.

Once we have determined to rescue our marriage, and have recognized before God and our spouse our full responsibility for the existing problems, this is the next step.

What do I mean by "exercise your faith"? When we first heard the Gospel, it was music to our ears. When we knew it was possible to be born again, changed, cleansed from sin, etc. we made a determination. We started believing for it. And indeed, that is the only way new life in Christ is received— by believing. Everything God has for us is received by believing.

If we are sick and we hear God's promise of healing and know that He healed all who came to Him, we begin to believe for it. This believing bears fruit. We get healed.

We receive the baptism of the Holy Spirit by faith. We exercise the gifts of the Spirit by faith. Everything we do in God is done by faith. We even worship by faith.

But, what do we mean by "exercise your faith"?

On one side we have the promises of God. On the other side we have the lies of Satan, the uncaring and doubtful comments of people around us, and our own negative thoughts. The carnal mind, the Scripture tells us, is the enemy of God (Romans 8:7).

When the faith of Adam and Eve was tested, they had God's Word on one side — that He loved them, had provided everything they needed, but required of them obedience to be demonstrated in the simple act of refraining from eating the fruit of a certain tree. On the other side they had Satan's lie — that God was just being petty, feared that the two of them would themselves become gods, and that the result of eating the fruit of the forbidden tree would not be bad (as God had indicated), but good. We know, lamentably, which party they chose to believe.

Exercising your faith means putting it into practice. Adam and Eve may have thought they loved God and believed Him. Their actions, however, were actions of unbelief. You must act in faith. You must think faith. You must talk faith.

I don't mean you pretend. If you believe God — that He is going to help you — you start thinking differently (Philippians 4:8-9). Negative thoughts are not of God. Thoughts that you are a failure are not of God. Thoughts that your life is ruined are not of God. Thoughts that all is lost are not of God. Thoughts that your situation cannot be turned around are not of God. You must reject such thoughts and start thinking God's thoughts.

Filling your mind with His promises will help. Read and memorize God's promises for marriage. Plant them into your spirit. Know that God wants you to be happy in your marriage. Know that God wants your marriage to be a foretaste of heaven. Know that God wants your marriage to teach you about the marvelous relationship you will have with Him throughout eternity. Push other thoughts aside. Don't listen to the negative comments of friends or family. Think God's thoughts.

When you start thinking God's thoughts, you start talking differently. Don't ever talk about divorce. Talk positive talk. Talk about good times. Don't ever drag up old problems. Let them lie buried. Talk about good times.

When you start thinking God's thoughts, you start acting differently. You are not acting out failure. You are acting out success. You stop planning for the worst and start planning for the best. You stop accepting the ultimate failure of your marriage and start celebrating its ultimate success. Start expecting a miracle. Faith is expecting.

I can never forget the inspired words of an Indian pastor I heard in my youth: "When faith goes to market, it always takes a basket!" That is exercising faith. Take a basket. Stop acting like a defeatist. Stop talking about divorce. Start planning your future. Start living your future.

Fear is the opposite of faith. It is a terribly debilitating force which opens the door to Satan. I know what I am talking about. When we began experiencing marital conflict, a terrible fear took hold of me, a terror of spending the rest of my life alone. Satan had found the spot where he could do me irrepable damage, and I seemed to be powerless to prevent it. That terrified me.

Fear set us on edge. It causes us to react wrongly to other people. It causes us to say and do things we are later sorry for. Fear is destructive.

Faith is constructive. When I had enough of the enemy's lies about my marriage and started believing God's promises, things quickly turned around. Faith in God is such a powerful force. Nothing can stand against us — when we believe.

This is not a time for depression, this is a time for optimism. There is nothing to be discouraged about, there is everything to be encouraged about. There is no reason to look back, there is every reason to look forward. God is on the throne. He hasn't lost His power. He has a wonderful future prepared for us. Don't disappoint Him by accepting second best. Exercise your faith in a positive way and reach out in expectancy for the miracles of God to be performed in your behalf. God never disappoints faith.

Chapter 5

Develop A Team Spirit

Marriage is a partnership, an equal partnership. It is not composed of one boss and one employee, one master and one slave, one executive and one laborer. Much has been taught in recent years of the biblical teaching of women's submission to their husbands. Few, however, have recognized that the Scriptures actually teach submission to each other — a team effort.

> *Submitting yourselves one to another in the fear of God.*
>
> Ephesians 5:21

Be subject one to another, and be clothed with
humility: for God resisteth the proud, and giveth
grace to the humble.

1 Peter 5:5

It isn't healthy for relationships to be one sided. It cannot be correct for our family to always eat what I like — just because I happen to be the husband and father in our household. If we are to exist along side other people, we cannot insist always on having our own way. Besides, we need to experience the variety we gain by trying other tastes.

For many years men ruled supreme over their households. No one was to question them. When they were asked why a certain thing was to be done in a certain way, their answer was invariably, "because I said so!" Now, women are rebelling against that heavy handedness and have gone the other way, taking upon themselves rights and privileges once reserved for their men. This has, of course, become a point of contention in the marriage.

God designed marriage so that both partners would be equal and each submitting to the other. There is great safety and enlargement in the mutual submission which the Scriptures envision. We are to love each other, and because of our love for each other, we are to protect each other, teach each other, warn each other, care for each other, provide for each other. Can we do less for each other than the Scriptures admonish us to do for any brother or sister in the faith? Here are some examples (in the order of their appearance) in the Word:

Be kindly affectioned one to another with brotherly love; in honour preferring one another;
Romans 12:10

Wherefore receive ye one another, as Christ also received us to the glory of God. Romans 15:7

With all lowliness and meekness, with longsuffering, forbearing one another in love; Ephesians 4:2

And be ye kind one to another, tenderhearted, forgiving one another, even as God for Christ's sake hath forgiven you. Ephesians 4:32

Forbearing one another, and forgiving one another, if any man have a quarrel against any: even as Christ forgave you, so also do ye.
Colossians 3:13

Let the word of Christ dwell in you richly in all wisdom; teaching and admonishing one another in psalms and hymns and spiritual songs, singing with grace in your hearts to the Lord.
Colossians 3:16

Wherefore comfort one another with these words.
1 Thessalonians 4:18

Wherefore comfort yourselves together, and edify one another, even as also ye do.
1 Thessalonians 5:11

*But **exhort one another** daily, while it is called To day; lest any of you be hardened through the deceitfulness of sin.*   Hebrews 3:13

*And let us **consider one another** to provoke unto love and to good works:*   Hebrews 10:24

*Not forsaking the assembling of ourselves together, as the manner of some is; but **exhorting one another**: and so much the more, as ye see the day approaching.*
                    Hebrews 10:25

***Confess your faults one to another**, and **pray one for another**, that ye may be healed. The effectual fervent prayer of a righteous man availeth much.*
                    James 5:16

*Seeing ye have purified your souls in obeying the truth through the spirit unto unfeigned love of the brethren, see that ye **love one another** with a pure heart fervently:*   1 Peter 1:22

***Use hospitality one to another** without grudging.*
                    1 Peter 4:9

*As every man hath received the gift, even so **minister** the same **one to another**, as good stewards of the manifold grace of God.*   1 Peter 4:10

*But if we walk in the light, as he is in the light, we **have fellowship one with another**, and the blood*

of Jesus Christ his Son cleanseth us from all sin.
1 John 1:7

*And this is his commandment, That we should believe on the name of his Son Jesus Christ, and **love one another**, as he gave us commandment.*
1 John 3:23

*Beloved, let us **love one another**: for love is of God; and every one that loveth is born of God, and knoweth God.*
1 John 4:7

There are specific things mentioned in Scripture that we are not to do to any brother or sister. So, we are not to do them to each other within the context of the marriage either:

*Let us **not** therefore **judge one another** any more: but judge this rather, that **no man put a stumblingblock or an occasion to fall in his brother's way**.*
Romans 14:13

*But if ye bite and devour one another, take heed that ye **be not consumed one of another**.*
Galatians 5:15

*Let us not be desirous of vain glory, **provoking one another, envying one another**.*
Galatians 5:26

***Lie not one to another**, seeing that ye have put off the old man with his deeds;*
Colossians 3:9

If we are meant to treat any of our Christian brothers and sisters with this respect and concern, how can we give less to our spouses? God has placed us in a bond of mutual love and respect. But, what about the definition of roles?

If we were meant to have totally defined roles, those roles would be more clearly spelled out in Scripture. They are not. Christian tradition has placed certain restraints on us. For example: that the man is *always* the bread winner of the family; the woman *always* stays home, etc. There are definite merits to these concepts, but they are not written in stone. We need to develop more flexible roles in the family based on the ability of each member and on mutual love and respect.

I believe there is one basic rule set down in Scripture. When God formed the family, He did not leave it without leadership. A body needs a head. A church needs a pastor. A company needs a president. A school needs a principal. God is not the author of confusion. He did not form anarchy. It is His clear design outlined in Scripture for man to accept the responsibility of headship in his home — with all that it suggests. "The buck stops here."

That does not mean the husband is the taskmaster over his little covey of slaves. It means he is servant of all. Jesus denounced the leadership style of the Pharisees (Matthew 23:1-7). They didn't do what they said. They were poor examples for others to follow. They expected too much of others and shirked their own responsibilities. What they did was for show. And they gloried in titles and in their place of honor.

Jesus denounced the leadership style of the gentiles. They *"exercised lordship"* over each other, using their position to personal advantage instead of serving. *"So shall it not be among you,"* Jesus said emphatically, *"but whosoever will be great among you, shall be your minister. And whosoever of you will be the chiefest, shall be servant of all"* (Mark 10:42-44). He set the example:

> *For even the Son of man came not to be ministered unto, but to minister, and to give His life a ransom for many.*   Mark 10:45

The role of the husband is to give himself for his wife. The role of the father is to give himself for his children. Most women don't have a problem with that kind of spirit. As the twenty-first century dawns, women are not about to be beaten into submission, but they will respond to mutual love and respect.

The role of the wife is not a lesser role. The role of the mother is not a lesser role. It is just a different role. And look carefully at the classic biblical example of a godly woman:

> *Who can find a virtuous woman? for her price is far above rubies. The heart of her husband doth safely trust in her, so that he shall have no need of spoil. She will do him good and not evil all the days of her life. She seeketh wool, and flax, and worketh willingly with her hands. She is like the merchants' ships; she bringeth her food from afar. She riseth also while it is yet night, and giveth meat to her household, and a portion to her maidens.*

*She considereth a field, and buyeth it: with the fruit
of her hands she planteth a vineyard. She girdeth her
loins with strength, and strengtheneth her arms. She
perceiveth that her merchandise is good: her candle
goeth not out by night. She layeth her hands to the
spindle, and her hands hold the distaff.*

*She stretcheth out her hand to the poor; yea, she
reacheth forth her hands to the needy. She is not
afraid of the snow for her household: for all her
household are clothed with scarlet. She maketh herself
coverings of tapestry; her clothing is silk and purple.*

*Her husband is known in the gates, when he sitteth
among the elders of the land. She maketh fine linen,
and selleth it; and delivereth girdles unto the merchant.
Strength and honour are her clothing; and she shall
rejoice in time to come. She openeth her mouth with
wisdom; and in her tongue is the law of kindness. She
looketh well to the ways of her household, and eateth
not the bread of idleness.*
*Her children arise up, and call her blessed; her
husband also, and he praiseth her. Many daughters
have done virtuously, but thou excellest them all.
Favour is deceitful, and beauty is vain: but a woman
that feareth the Lord, she shall be praised. Give her
of the fruit of her hands; and let her own works praise
her in the gates.*   Proverbs 31:10-31

This woman is not sitting home watching soap operas.
She "has" it all. She is a business woman. She is buying

lands and planting crops. She is buying materials and producing from them a product which she sells to the merchants. She finds time to minister to the poor. She manages all that without neglecting the individual needs of the members of her family. She takes personal responsibility for her children.

Yet, her husband doesn't feel intimidated by all this. He doesn't feel less of a man because his wife does so much. He is rightfully proud of her. And his family's well-being gives him a respect that enables him to sit on the council and decide matters which affect the entire community.

This situation clearly is not typical of every marriage. Not every man has a higher calling to serve the community at large. The average man must work for the welfare of his immediate family. Yet, this is clearly God's kind of woman. She is capable. She is caring. She is respected and trusted by her husband and children. They *"rise up and call her blessed."*

I still marvel at the schedule Diane kept for several years while we were living in Quito, Ecuador. She is an early riser. Before I got up to go to prayer and start the activities of the Bible School and missions office, she was up preparing breakfast and getting the children off to school. After they were gone, she set about to clean the house and do the laundry. The house was always well kept. By ten she was in the mission office ready for a day spent with government officials of that Latin country, clearing materials from customs, securing visas for missionaries, working for building permits, travel papers. She did most of the buying.

By three thirty she was back in the house to receive the children when they got home from school. Dinner was prepared. And never once in those years did any member of the family miss the regular church activities it was our responsibility to attend and participate in. She was never "too tired."

And I didn't mention helping the children with their homework, participating in the activities of the school, etc.

Women are extremely capable people. They are not lesser creatures. Why should we be intimidated by a strong woman? We should be glad to have them on our team.

At the opposite end of the spectrum we have women who are engaged in male bashing these days. They delight in putting their husbands down, in getting the best of them however they can. They seem to be saying, "Let's do to them what they did to us for so many years." There is certainly nothing Christian about this spirit.

Avoid these two extremes. Make your marriage a team effort. Develop a healthy respect for your mate, and determine to live with each other in cooperation.

I believe that a husband and father, if he is a believer, should set long term goals for the family and overall guidelines for attaining those goals. That leaves plenty of room, however, for the creativity and participation of every other member of the family in the pursuit of those goals. If the man of the house lays down the law about every step that must be taken and exactly how that step must be taken (because he always knows best), he stifles the entire family and causes rebellion.

Men, if you want your wives to submit to you, love them like Christ loved the Church (Ephesians 5:25). Don't force your will on them.

Don't struggle over who is going to spend "my money." If the wife is better at paying the bills or has more time to do it, she should — no matter who "makes" the money. Keeping the man always in the role of bread-winner and the woman as the housewife has given the husband many unfair advantages. Men have been guilty of trying to control the marriage and limit their mates authority through money. No wonder many women are desperate to earn their own money. Let your authority come from genuine respect, not from contrived circumstances.

Don't struggle over who is to guide the children. Do it TOGETHER.

Don't struggle over family activities. Make those decisions TOGETHER. This is a team. Get some teamwork going. Pass the ball around. Every member of the team is important. We are going to win this thing together.

Recent studies asked a variety of workers what they wanted most from their jobs. Far above salary and benefits and advancement came "respect and appreciation." Take the hint.

Chapter 6

Keep Working At It

What are you waiting for? Get busy. There is no time to lose. Nothing worthwhile just happens, you have to work at it.

"What do I do?" I hear you ask.

How did you win your wife in the first place? With surprises of flowers? By taking her out to eat? By doing unexpected chores for her?

How did you win your husband in the first place? Start courting him again. Go ahead, it's fun! If you hadn't stopped courting and taken everything for granted, you wouldn't be in the jam you are in right now. Marriage is meant to be exciting, like the courting days. It is meant to be fun, like the courting days.

It doesn't matter how many children you have already. Don't let children take the romance out of marriage.

It doesn't matter how much work you each have to do. Our business responsibilities should not be permitted to hinder our marital life.

It doesn't matter how tired you are. Getting older doesn't mean you have to stop having fun. Have some fun! Have some excitement! Do some courting!

Most of us did some serious courting with someone who was not the least bit interested in our attentions, but that didn't stop us. I didn't say this was going to be easy. I didn't say this was going to be mutual. It may not be. But, whatever is worth having is worth fighting for. It is worth striving for. It is worth sacrificing for. And your marriage is worth whatever effort is necessary.

What was involved in your first courtship? Telephone calls? Visits? Flowers? Dinners together? Take whatever time is necessary. You have nothing more important to do, nothing more urgent. Push some other things aside. Make room on your calendar for courting. Don't worry about what people are saying. Don't worry about how it looks. Just have a good time. Enjoy yourself.

You will experience some setbacks. Don't be shaken by them. You will experience some hard places. Don't be discouraged. Keep the goal in mind. Keep God's promises in mind. Keep your faith high. One bad note does not ruin a symphony. Keep working at it.

How long should you keep working at it? As long as it takes!

To what lengths should you be willing to go? Whatever it takes!

Why is it that we are so willing to work hard and train for a job and we are so unwilling to put forth an effort to rescue our marriages? Something is wrong here.

We spend so many years preparing for a career, yet we are so unprepared to be mates and parents. We expect to be instant successes with a minimum of effort. It doesn't happen that way.

As this book goes to press, Diane and I are celebrating our twenty-fifth wedding anniversary. With God's help we rescued our marriage from certain destruction and have learned a lot through the years. Our love and respect for one another has grown. We have found great happiness together. We do not, however, yet have the perfect marriage. We are still learning, and we are still working at it.

So, get busy. Don't delay any longer. You're fighting for your life here. You are fighting for your soul here. Don't tire of the effort. KEEP WORKING AT IT!

Chapter 7

Allow Time for Healing

Since the marriage relationship is the most intimate of all relationships, in marriage we open ourselves to the deepest hurts. When there are serious difficulties in the marriage, usually there are hurts on both sides that produce a rupture and complicate everything. We say and do many things for which we are later sorry. Deep hurt creates a volatile situation and can lead to violence.

Once you have realized that your marriage is worth rescuing, have asked God to help you get your thinking about marriage straightened out, have taken full responsibility for the past, have begun to exercise your faith in a positive way, have recognized the importance of developing a team spirit, and have started making whatever effort necessary to correct the errors of the past, allow time for healing.

There must be a cooling-off period. It may take a few weeks, it may take a few months, or it may actually take as long as a year or more. During this time, it is not a good idea to be separated, a mistake that many make. By separating, you open yourself up to temptation and bring further grief upon the marriage. Stay together and, if necessary, keep your mouth shut. Simply avoid the discussion of those things which cause controversy. There will be time later for discussing everything at length.

Suffer whatever wrongs are done to you during this time — in faith that time heals all wounds. It won't "kill" you, and you'll be a better person for it.

It is during this healing period that the intervention of a third party is probably helpful. A third party will not take sides, will demand that both have a chance to speak and that both listen to the other. Sometimes they need do nothing more. A third party helps to keep tempers in check while we endeavor to understand a point of view that we have either failed to understand or refused to understand. A third party helps to keep things in perspective.

Emotions are high. We say unreasonable things, hurtful things. It is hard for us to see things in a rational way. We look at everything through the overlay of hurt pride, failure, embarrassment etc. The third party can be invaluable — but, not just any third party!

Israel was ruled by judges who were wise and anointed servants of God. The judge would listen carefully to both parties in a land dispute, a case of inheritance, a marital feud etc, would take the case before the Lord, and would come back with a suggested solution.

We need more such people in the church today. Counseling is (for the most part) a pseudo-ministry in which carnal techniques are used to guide God's people. This is an abomination. God wants to resolve our problems in His way. Seek out a wise and prayerful servant of God.

Seek an unbiased person, one who will not be scandalized by the revelations of marital strife, one who will not use the knowledge they gain to hurt you more. Believe God for a miracle in this respect.

There may be subjects that you will have to avoid for quite some time. If you notice a bristling or feel a change in the atmosphere, just back off for a while. There are more important things. If it involves money, let it go. If it involves your "rights," give them up. Go the extra mile (Matthew 5:41).

Young people are very idealistic and drive hard toward their ideals. Maturity doesn't have to mean a loss of idealism. It does mean, however, a more realistic approach to life. None of us are perfect. If we are to live together, we must respect and understand other viewpoints.

There is a certain healing mechanism built into the human body. When a person is wounded or becomes ill, a whole series of bodily functions kick in to fight the infection and disease and return the body to normal health. The whole of nature is blessed by this healing gift of God. If a destroyed environment is discovered in time and left alone, it heals itself and restores itself to normal health. What a wonderful miracle of God!

God has built into the marriage the same restorative powers. Given a proper atmosphere, the proper rest, the proper nourishment etc., marriages heal.

If you break a bone, you must give it time to heal. When it does heal it is stronger, we are told, than before. The same is true of a marriage. A restored marriage is a strong marriage. A restored marriage is a tough marriage. A restored marriage is resistant to the diseases and infections that once nearly took its life. It just needs time to heal, time without further affliction of pain, time without further twisting and turning, time to rest, time to enjoy, time to be at peace.

Someday you will be able to look back and smile at this moment, but it is not funny now. It is a very painful process. It is, however, worth the wait, worth the effort. The alternative is not attractive. So, go for it!

Let God save your marriage. He instituted it. He made the blueprint. When something is wrong, He knows what it is and how to fix it. He will heal your marriage — if you give Him a chance. Be patient! Allow time for healing.

Chapter 8

A Word About "The Big Three"

Psychologists and counselors tell us that three things repeatedly pop up in marriage counseling: money, sex and communication. They are the three most common sources of conflict in marriage. While I agree that money, sex and communication are three very important elements of any marriage and can be sources of conflict in the relationship , I am afraid that we are looking for a quick fix for marriage — as we do for most everything else these days. And I don't believe a quick fix exists for marriage.

I think, therefore, that the overwhelming emphasis placed on the "big three" in recent years may have sidetracked us from the more fundamental issues at hand and actually prolonged or weakened the healing process.

To concentrate on these three areas as a "solution" to marital problems is, I believe, getting the proverbial cart before the horse.

Money

What could be more important than money? It represents our life, our time, our talent, our work. It is extremely important. Jesus showed us that God is concerned with our correct stewardship of money when He took time from His busy schedule to sit near the Temple offering box and point out to the disciples the miserly giving of the rich and the generous giving of the widow (Mark 12:41-44).

Every believer must learn to handle money in a way that is pleasing to God. And, in the context of the marriage (because it has the potential for causing jealousy and misunderstanding), we must learn to handle money WISELY and TOGETHER.

But, money is not the reason marriages fail.

Did you fight over money when your were courting? I doubt it. And you probably had very little money then. When you love each other, everything can be resolved. It is when the glow wears off that jealousies and resentments enter over who handles the money and what your spending priorities are. You could have any amount of money and this problem would not be resolved.

Looking to money as a cause and a solution is the same mistake men have been making for centuries. Most inhabitants of the poorer countries believe that if they could somehow get to live in America, their problems would be over. This is one of Satan's classic lies. Yet, daily they pour across our borders in search of the hidden treasure. Many families are destroyed by what they wrongly see as a solution to their problems.

Recognize the importance of money and its correct use, and work together to please God with your finances. But, don't look to money to solve your marital problems. Instead, get that divine flow of love moving again, and you will be able to work out together any financial difficulties you might encounter.

Almost everyone experiences the problem of wanting more than they can afford. "Easy payment" plans have placed nearly everyone in a bind at one time or another. If your personal relationship were more fulfilling, maybe you wouldn't be so driven to acquire "things." The bills are not always the real problem, many times it is the problems that produce the bills.

The coming of the children add financial pressures to any family. Yet the joy they bring us and the satisfaction of seeing in physical form the result of our mutual love override any negative financial aspects. We can make the necessary adjustments. We can make the necessary sacrifices. We can work hard. We can do all this and more — if our love is strong. Finances become a point of conflict only if that love is not kept fresh.

Don't look for the quick fix. Work out your marital difficulties in God's way and with His help.

Sex

Sex is important. The physical attraction between a man and wife is one of the glues that hold the family together. Human sexuality is unlike any other in the animal kingdom.

Some animals multiply without the help of a mate. Fish need only the fertilization of the male on the eggs. Then, both male and female leave the eggs to hatch and fend for themselves. In a very few animal species the male and female unite for life. Even then, they have sex only in periods of procreation. The human female is unique in that she is able to have sexual relations at any time.

The male animal is motivated by scents generated only at mating intervals, while the human male is motivated by the mere presence of his loved one, by the very thought of her — any time. This definitely helps to keep him around.

A young calf doesn't need the father anymore. Young ducks, within a very few weeks are able to fend for themselves. Some male birds take turns warming the nest or guarding the young. But, their work is short-lived. Within just a few weeks the little ones are out of the nest flying about on their own.

The human male is needed permanently, by his mate and by his children. He is held to them by both the emotional and physical attraction.

Most males (in the animal kingdom), once the physical attraction is satisfied, leave. Others must be driven away by the females to protect the young. Among mammals, mothers are bound to their young ones by their need of milk. The father has no such binding. He may protect the herd, but does little more.

Sex is important. Don't relegate it to the back burner. But, don't fall for the media hype. The product is highly overrated. A lot more than good sex is needed in a happy marriage.

And how is good sex achieved? Is it the result of some technique? Will a certain type of kiss turn your partner on?

The technique used in love-making is not nearly as important as developing trust and mutual respect. When you love someone you intuitively do the things that please them. You develop your own technique. Nobody else's technique will do for your marriage. But, with it all, don't expect too much. Sex was never intended to be a cure all.

Sex must be an integral part of a happy marriage. But, sex is not the cause of the problems in a marriage, nor is it the solution. The problem is not the sex, but what is making the sex unsatisfying or nonexistent. When love grows cold, sex grows stale, mechanical. Revive the love and expect the sex to get better with age. You won't be disappointed.

Communication

Communication is a skill that all of us need to learn and keep learning. Understanding our fellow man has

never been easy. Even with two people who are married
to each other, it is almost as if we spoke different lan-
guages. Understanding each other requires not only
saying things in a clear way, but also listening carefully
to what the other person is saying (This requires reading
the emotions, as well, for we often don't say what we
mean).

The singular token of praise that most everyone had
for President Reagan was to recognize his skill as "the
great communicator."

Communication skills are needed for our jobs and for
all of our other relationships in life. Many of us are just
now learning to effectively communicate our love to the
Lord Jesus. We have much to learn about the subject.

It seems absurd to me, however, that so many counselors consider "lack of communication" to be the major
cause of marriage breakups. "Your problem is a 'lack of
communication' " has become a pat answer given to
every couple — whatever their problem.

One respected Christian counselor quotes "a twelve
year old study" that shows that of couples interviewed,
those who said they communicated well had happy
marriages, and those who said they didn't communicate
well also said they had unhappy marriages.

Well, of course they don't communicate well. What
should we expect? When you believe that the person you
committed your future to has betrayed you, it becomes
difficult for you to communicate well with them. When
it becomes apparent that the person who knows you
better than anyone else in this world no longer trusts

you, that doesn't make for the best of conversations. When the person to whom you have opened yourself up emotionally and before whom you have become vulnerable hurts you, no longer cares for you, misinterprets everything you say, and wants to leave you and take away your children, you are not always ready to "hear" what they are saying.

What do we expect? Do you have good communications with your enemies? Do you have good communications with a business rival? Do you have good communications with a competitor?

Is "lack of communications" the cause of wars? Of course there is a "lack of communication" in war. Your enemy is trying to kill you. There cannot be proper communications when there is no proper relationship.

Saying that a "lack of communication" is the problem is like saying that a child became ill with measles because red bumps came up all over their body. The red bumps are not the cause of the sickness, only a symptom, the result of the sickness.

So, a "lack of communication" is not the problem with your marriage. Get the relationship straightened out and the communication will immediately improve. Then, work at theses skills.

It is so easy to misunderstand each other that we must be constantly improving our communication skills. Don't tire of the effort. It will bring its rewards. This is the person you love. This is the person you married. This is the person to whom you made a life-time commitment. Don't give up on them. Don't write them off. Give them the time and attention they need and deserve. Give them the respect and courtesy you expect for yourself.

But, please don't simply brush your problems off as "a lack of communication." Probably that will be the next no fault divorce requirement.

"Why are you filing for divorce?"

"Irreconcilable differences!"

"Why are you filing for divorce?"

"Lack of communication."

Let THE Great Communicator put the spark back in your life and restore your respect and common consideration for each other.

Many other things that we think of as causes of our unhappiness with the marriage are really only symptoms of our lost love. When a mate has no desire at all to do things that please, is preoccupied with other things, dedicates himself/herself and his/her time more to the children, these are not causes of marital problems. These are only the symptoms. When the flame burns afresh externals will change.

It would be a mistake not to try to improve in any area that we are lacking. For example, when we have fevers, we know that an underlying sickness is probably to blame. We treat the fever, however, knowing that doing so will contribute to our eventual healing. Work on all your points of conflict. Any way that you can show your mate your true concern for the relationship and for him or her as a person can only help bring about a total restoration.

As you listen better, respect his/her opinion (even when you don't agree, etc. God is working on the underlying issue — the renewal of that Divine love.

Never lose sight of this key element. Let God pour in a fresh supply. A restored marriage is a miracle from the hand of a loving Father. EXPECT A MIRACLE!

Chapter 9

The Spoiler

I intended to end the book at this point since I didn't want it to get "heavy." I wanted it to be a joyous book. I wanted people to read it and feel light, encouraged and hopeful. And, I wanted the book to be short so that more busy people would read it. I never intended it to cover every detail of every situation. I wanted it to establish a base to work from, nothing more.

I was preparing a final chapter which I intended to call, "God's Viewpoint on Marriage" or "Marriage From God's Perspective." It was nothing more than a detailed outline of the Bible teaching on marriage. [Much of it now can be found in the Appendix A, *Biblical Gems Concerning Marriage.*]

As I went over and over that outline for a number of days, perfecting it, I could not escape the truth that I had left out something very important. My omission became so glaring to me that I had to add this final chapter.

From the beginning of time, one element has kept intruding on God's perfect plan for marriage — for the patriarchs, for the kings of Israel, for men of all degree and of all generations. That element is SIN. I simply couldn't close the book without saying something about that terrible spoiler.

Marriage was conceived and established by God.

> *And the Lord God said, It is not good that the man should be alone; I will make him an help meet for him. And the Lord God caused a deep sleep to fall upon Adam, and he slept: and He took one of his ribs, and closed up the flesh instead thereof; And the rib which the Lord God had taken from man, made He a woman, and brought here unto man. And Adam said, This now bone of my bones, and flesh of my flesh: she shall be called Woman, because she was taken out of Man. Therefore shall a man leave his father and his mother, and shall cleave unto his wife: and they shall be one flesh.*
>
> Genesis 2:18 & 21-24

God designed marriage as a mystical union which is a type of our eventual union with Him in eternity. As such marriage should be a foretaste of that glory.

> *For this cause shall a man leave his father and mother, and shall be joined unto his wife, and they*

two shall be one flesh. This is a great mystery: but I speak concerning Christ and the Church.
Ephesians 5:31-32

Marriage, then, should be the nearest thing to heaven that we can experience on this earth. Once we get to heaven, there will be no further need of marriage — because there we will experience the perfect joy of union with God.

For in the resurrection they neither marry, nor are given in marriage, but are as the angels of God in heaven.   Matthew 22:30

For when they shall rise from the dead, they neither marry, nor are given in marriage; but are as the angels which are in heaven.   Mark 12:25

Throughout Scripture God used the comparison of the husband-wife relationship to express His desired relationship to His people.

Turn, O backsliding children, saith the Lord; for I am married unto you.   Jeremiah 3:14

Not according to the covenant that I made with their fathers in the day that I took them by the hand to bring them out of the land of Egypt; which my covenant they brake, although I was an husband unto them, saith the Lord: Jeremiah 31:32

> *For I am jealous over you with godly jealousy: for I
> have espoused you to one husband, that I may present
> you as a chaste virgin to Christ.*
>   2 Corinthians 11:2

Since marriage was meant to be glorious, God didn't
question whether man would or would not choose to live
with his designated companion in this state of near
heaven. *"Therefore shall a man...,"* He said. Why wouldn't
anyone want to experience this joy? God placed a
natural desire in man's heart for this companionship
and established marriage as the normal and correct
thing to do. This is God's plan. Those who would, *"in the
latter times,"* forbid marriage, God's Word warns us, are
"depart[ing] from the faith," and *"giving heed to seducing
spirits and doctrines of devils"* (1 Timothy 4:1-3).

Marriage is of God and is recommended by Scripture
as *"good"* and *"honourable."*

> *Whoso findeth a wife findeth a good thing, and
> obtaineth favour of the Lord.*   Proverbs 18:22

> *Marriage is honourable in all, and the bed undefiled:
> but whoremongers and adulterers God will judge.*
>   Hebrews 13:4

Married people are seen by God (and by bankers) as
more stable, complete, and fulfilled people.

> *Let the deacons be the husbands of one wife, ruling
> their children and their own houses well.*
>   1 Timothy 3:12

God instructed men and women alike to take marriage seriously. It was not to be entered into lightly nor broken lightly.

What therefore God hath joined together, let not man put asunder.   Mark 10:9

For the woman which hath an husband is bound by the law to her husband so long as he liveth.
Romans 7:2

And unto the married I command, yet not I, but the Lord, Let not the wife depart from her husband:
1 Corinthians 7:10

Let not the husband put away his wife.
1 Corinthians 7:11

No sooner had God established this miraculous and mystical union of man and wife, this potentially heavenly relationship, than men and women began looking for ways to get out, to circumvent God's plan — one man for one woman, one woman for one man. Something tragic happened to spoil the perfection that God intended for the relationship. Marriage was not only taken lightly, it was resented as being restrictive. Men and women alike began abusing marriage and breaking its sacred vows.

The sin of Adam and Eve — their rebellion against God and their choice to believe the tempter rather than the Creator — spoiled God's perfect design for their lives and for all succeeding generations. Sin became the great spoiler. And because man did not maintain the proper relationship with His God, his relationship to his mate became corrupted as well.

God created men and women equal, to share together His blessings.

> *And God said, Let us make man in Our image, after Our likeness: So God created man in His own image, in the image of God created He him; male and female created He them. And God blessed them ... .*
> Genesis 1:26-28

Sin brought the marriage partners into conflict, into competition. They began to use each other for selfish ends — rather than complementing each other and bringing joy to each other, as God intended.

Marriage became a political tool. Marrying into the right family was advantageous in forming alliances with unfriendly neighbors.

Marriage became a financial tool. Fathers decided to charge a dowry for their fairest daughters, making them little more than chattel to be traded for livestock or other forms of wealth.

As He did to protect other sacred things, God made laws to protect the sanctity of marriage. The most important of those laws forbid the children of Israel from marrying pagans (unbelievers) because their attitude toward marriage was so different than His own.

Lest ... thou take of their daughters unto thy sons, and their daughters go a whoring after their gods, and make thy sons go a whoring after their gods.
                                         Exodus 34:15-16

Neither shalt thou make marriages with them; thy daughter thou shalt not give unto his son, nor his daughter shalt thou take unto thy son. For they will turn away thy son from following Me, that they may serve other gods: so will the anger of the Lord be kindled against you, and destroy thee suddenly.
                                          Deuteronomy 7:3-4

Take good heed therefore unto yourselves, that ye love the Lord your God. Else if ye do in any wise go back, and cleave unto the remnant of these nations, even these that remain among you, and shall make marriages with them, and go in unto them, and they to you ... They will be snares and traps unto you ... .
                                            Joshua 23:11-13

God knew what He was doing. Since marriage is His design, only those who know and love Him can understand its purpose and experience its true potential. As usual, however, not everyone believed what God said:

And the children of Israel dwelt among the Canaanites, Hittites, and Amorites, and Perizzites, and Hivites, and Jebusites: And they took their daughters to be their wives, and gave their daughters to their sons, and served their gods. And the children of Israel did evil in the sight of the Lord, and forgat the Lord their God, and served Baalim and the groves. Therefore the anger of the Lord was hot against Israel, and He sold them into the hand of Chushanrishathaim king of Mesopotamia: and the children of Israel served Chushanrishathaim eight years. Judges 3:5-8

The saddest case on record was that of the very "wise" King Solomon.

But king Solomon loved many strange women, together with the daughter of Pharaoh, women of the Moabites, Ammonites, Edomites, Zidonians, and Hittites: Of the nations concerning which the Lord said unto the children of Israel, Ye shall not go in to them, neither shall they come in unto you: for surely they will turn away your heart after their gods: Solomon clave unto these in love. And he had seven hundred wives, princesses, and three hundred concubines: and his wives turned away his heart. For it came to pass, when Solomon was old, that his wives turned away his heart after other gods: and his heart was not perfect with the Lord his God, as was the heart of David his father. For Solomon went after Ashtoreth the goddess of the Zidonians, and after Milcom the abomination of the Ammonites. And Solomon did evil in the sight of the Lord, and went not fully after the Lord, as did David his father. Then did Solomon build an high place for Chemosh, the abomination of Moab, in the hill that is before Jerusalem, and for Molech, the abomination of the

children of Ammon. And likewise did he for all his
strange wives, which burnt incense and sacrificed
unto their gods. And the Lord was angry with
Solomon, because his heart was turned from the Lord
God of Israel, which had appeared unto him twice,
And had commanded him concerning this thing, that
he should not go after other gods: but he kept not that
which the Lord commanded. Wherefore the Lord said
unto Solomon, Forasmuch as this is done of thee, and
thou hast not kept My covenant and My statutes,
which I have commanded thee, I will surely rend the
kingdom from thee, and will give it to thy servant.
Notwithstanding in thy days I will not do it for David
thy father's sake: but I will rend it out of the hand of
thy son.   1 Kings 11:1-12

Avoiding his terrible mistake became one of the major
themes of Solomon's proverbs:

To deliver thee from the strange woman, even from
the stranger which flattereth with her words; Which
forsaketh the guide of her youth, and forgetteth the
covenant of her God.   Proverbs 2:16-17

For the lips of a strange woman drop as an honeycomb,
and her mouth is smoother than oil: But her end is
bitter as wormwood, sharp as a two-edged sword.
Her feet go down to death; her steps take hold on hell.
Lest thou shouldest ponder the path of life, her ways
are moveable, that thou canst not know them.
                                         Proverbs 5:3-6

*Remove thy way far from her, and come not nigh the
door of her house:Lest thou give thine honour unto
others, and thy years unto the cruel: Lest strangers be
filled with thy wealth; and thy labours be in the house
of a stranger; And thou mourn at the last, when thy
flesh and thy body are consumed,*

Proverbs 5:8-11

*Drink waters out of thine own cistern, and running
waters out of thine own well. Let thy fountains be
dispersed abroad, and rivers of waters in the streets.
Let them be only thine own, and not strangers' with
thee. Let thy fountain be blessed: and rejoice with the
wife of thy youth. Let her be as the loving hind and
pleasant roe; let her breasts satisfy thee at all times;
and be thou ravished always with her love.*

Proverbs 5:15-19

*To keep thee from the evil woman, from the flattery
of the tongue of a strange woman. Lust not after her
beauty in thine heart; neither let her take thee with her
eyelids. For by means of a whorish woman a man is
brought to a piece of bread: and the adulteress will
hunt for the precious life. Can a man take fire in his
bosom, and his clothes not be burned?*

Proverbs 6:24-27

*My son, keep my words, and lay up my commandments
with thee. That they may keep thee from the strange
woman, from the stranger which flattereth with her
words.*   Proverbs 7:1 & 5

*For a whore is a deep ditch; and a strange woman is
a narrow pit.*   Proverbs 23:27

The case of Solomon was so sad, not only because of
his renowned wisdom, but because he also gave Israel
some of the greatest expressions of God's undying love
in his *Song of Songs*. It not only teaches us how much God
loves us, but how He longs for our love in return.

*Tell me, O thou whom my soul loveth, where thou
feedest, where thou makest thy flock to rest at noon:
for why should I be as one that turneth aside by the
flocks of thy companions? If thou know not, O thou
fairest among women, go thy way forth by the
footsteps of the flock, and feed thy kids beside the
shepherds' tents. I have compared thee, O my love, to
a company of horses in Pharaoh's chariots. Thy
cheeks are comely with rows of jewels, thy neck with
chains of gold. We will make thee borders of gold with
studs of silver.*   Song of Solomon 1:7-11

Israel never forgot the case of Solomon.

*In those days also saw I Jews that had married wives
of Ashdod, of Ammon, and of Moab: And their
children spake half in the speech of Ashdod, and
could not speak in the Jews' language, but according
to the language of each people. And I contended with
them, and cursed them, and smote certain of them,
and plucked off their hair, and made them swear by
God, saying, Ye shall not give your daughters unto*

their sons, nor take their daughters unto your sons,
or for yourselves. Did not Solomon king of Israel sin
by these things? yet among many nations was there no
king like him, who was beloved of his God, and God
made him king over all Israel: nevertheless even him
did outlandish women cause to sin. Shall we then
hearken unto you to do all this great evil, to transgress
against our God in marrying strange wives?
                                                    Nehemiah 13:23-27

The unmistakable conclusion of those who study
God's Word is that marriage, if it is to conform to God's
perfect plan, must be *"only in the Lord."*

The wife is bound by the law as long as her husband
liveth; but if her husband be dead, she is at liberty to
be married to whom she will; only in the Lord.
                                                    1 Corinthians 7:39

Be ye not unequally yoked together with unbelievers:
for what fellowship hath righteousness with
unrighteousness? and what communion hath light
with darkness? And what concord hath Christ with
Belial? or what part hath he that believeth with an
infidel? And what agreement hath the temple of God
with idols? for ye are the temple of the living God; as
God hath said, I will dwell in them, and walk in
them; and I will be their God, and they shall be my
people. Wherefore come out from among them, and
be ye separate, saith the Lord, and touch not the
unclean thing; and I will receive you.
                                                    2 Corinthians 6:14-17

Marriage is so sacred that it must be protected:

I wrote unto you in an epistle not to company with fornicators: 1 Corinthians 5:9

Know ye not that your bodies are the members of Christ? shall I then take the members of Christ, and make them the members of an harlot? God forbid.
                                                1 Corinthians 6:15

Flee also youthful lusts: but follow righteousness, faith, charity, peace, with them that call on the Lord out of a pure heart.   2 Timothy 2:22

But now I have written unto you not to keep company, if any man that is called a brother be a fornicator, or covetous, or an idolater, or a railer, or a drunkard, or an extortioner; with such an one no not to eat.   1 Corinthians 5:11

Jesus' own teaching about marriage was preceded by the words, *"Except your righteousness shall exceed the righteousness of the scribes and Pharisees, ye shall in no case enter into the kingdom of heaven"* (Matthew 5:20). Unrighteousness, sin, any kind of sin, will damage the marriage relationship.

How could a man as wise as Solomon make such tragic mistakes in his life? The only conclusion we can reach is that the prevailing attitude about marriage in the world in which he lived was so attractive to him that he was deceived by it. Think about that! One of the wisest men who ever lived was deceived into believing that the pagan attitude toward marriage was harmless and even beneficial.

Should we be surprised that marriage is in trouble in the closing decade of the twentieth century? We are barraged on every side with the prevailing views of our time — views totally opposed to God's own as to the purpose of marriage, what is to be expected from marriage, the responsibilities of the marriage partners to each other, how we are to relate to each other etc. Much of the counseling being done with married couples who seek outside help is motivated by wrong concepts. What good results can be expected?

It is only by recognizing God's plan for marriage and by submitting ourselves totally to Him that we can realize the promised joys of this sacred institution. Only His wisdom and grace can help us solve our marital conflicts.

Turn to Him today, and EXPECT A MIRACLE!

Chapter 10

My Turn

by

Diane McDougal

Several times in recent years Harold has asked me to share the writing of this book. Since he is the writer in the family, I was hesitant. He went ahead with his portion and, with great thought and prayerful consideration, began to put pen to paper (in this case, fingertips to keyboard). When I read over what he had done, I got inspired to do my part.

I just wish that a similar book had been available to us when we were just starting out as a young Christian couple. I am sure it would have made us more aware of the pitfalls the enemy has placed before us and saved us many heartaches. Perhaps it was for the best, since our experiences have prepared us to write *"Rescuing the 21st Century Marriage."*

The greatest lie the enemy wants us to believe is that a Christian marriage will be easy. How can we go wrong? We have both dedicated our lives to the Lord. We are both born-again. We believe in miracles. We believe that two become one in the Lord. We all believe that nothing could possibly go wrong? Surely the standard fairy tale ending will prove to be true in our case: *"They all lived happily ever after."*

Pre-marital Misconceptions

We Christians enter marriage with a number of misconceptions and false expectations. The courtship years and the beauty and pageantry of the marriage ceremony leave us in that fairy tale atmosphere. The bride to be plans every minute detail: just the right wedding invitations, the perfect dress, the perfect colors, the perfect flowers, the perfect reception, the perfect honeymoon. What a rude awakening awaits us! Marriage is no fairy tale. This is the real world. We haven't reached perfection yet.

Imagine Jacob when he woke up in the morning looking into the face of Leah, not Rachel, whom he loved. When we take vows of marriage blindly, without counting the cost and recognizing the consequences, just such a rude awakening awaits us.

Post-marital Adjustments

During the first year of a marriage there is a "battle of identities" that all newlyweds experience. We've given up our freedom, committed to a lifelong union and a promise to share all of our worldly possessions. Up until now we have said and done all the right things, wanting to please the one we love. But after the wedding, the reality of it all has hit home. We suddenly feel as if we have no say over our lives. All the little incidentals and idiosyncrasies that we brushed off during courtship suddenly take on a whole new perspective. "This is the person I have committed my life to."

There are so many adjustments to be made in marriage. Becoming one in the flesh sounds so easy. It doesn't always prove to be as easy as it sounds. Two very different people (from two very different home situations, with two very different ways of thinking and reacting to life) living together in peace and harmony has to be a miracle. We're talking major adjustments here.

Any change in life requires adjustment: changes in your profession, changes in where you live, changes in your daily habits, etc. Harold and I did it all at once. We not only got married, we got married and worked in the ministry. We got married, and within months were on the mission field. We got married, and very soon were expecting our first child.

Adjusting to each other was hard enough. We had to adjust to a new climate, new foods, new living conditions, new friends, etc. Our life totally changed.

We have worked with so many young people through the years and seen so many of them fall in love and get married. Every single one of them lived in a surreal world of false expectations, never anticipating even the smallest quarrel with their chosen mate. And every one of them had their share of words to eat later.

Marriage is never what we expect it to be. We're under the myth that everything will be fine and take care of itself once we're married. Wrong! We need to work at marriage as well as anything else in life that is worth having. If we could enter marriage with this knowledge, we would save a lot of time and tears. Most couples wait until their marriage is in trouble before they begin to get serious and work at the relationship.

Marriage demands a totally different life style of us. It demands plenty of sacrifice on both sides. Adjustment takes time.

Children

The coming of the children not only is cause for further adjustment in our lives, it introduces a potentially divisive element into the marriage. That is a shame because there is no greater joy than parenthood and all the wonderful experiences and blessings it brings.

Because we had dedicated our lives to missions, we thought we would wait a while before having children.

We didn't prove too adept at birth control, however, and Debbie was born nine months and one day after we were married — just three weeks after we arrived in Manila, Philippines.

God knew what He was doing. Debbie was a source of great joy and comfort to us as we adjusted to our new surroundings and the absence of other family members. The Filipinos loved each of the children, who actually seemed to open doors of ministry to us and to ease our introduction to the nationals.

Something, however, happens to a woman when she becomes a "mommy" for the first time. She suddenly holds in her hands a tiny life, and it can be terrifying, for she has no prior experience. Yet, the Lord births within her a natural instinct for mothering. I found being a mother in the primitive surroundings of Southeast Asia to be a particularly challenging experience. Being a mother is a full time job. I had to get a lot of "on the job training." I had a few books to refer to, but the books could never convey the transformation that overcomes a woman upon motherhood. Motherhood causes you to grow up fast.

The coming of the children gives father his share of experiences and transformations, nevertheless the responsibility of continual care rests upon the mom. And with this new emotional responsibility we mothers so often, unaware of the dangers, neglect the fathers.

The danger is that the developing relationship with the child, necessarily time-consuming and at times exhausting, may begin to detract from the intimate

relationship we are attempting to build with our husbands. Changing diapers and feeding babies somehow
does not put us in a romantic mood. A woman needs to
be wooed and pampered through the day. Her involve-
ment with the children, however, leaves little time for
this wooing.

She often is "too busy" and brushes off her husbands
attentions, and if he is brushed off enough times, he
gives up trying. She then complains that he doesn't care
for her anymore and is only interested in sex. The truth
is that many times she is guilty of turning him away. As
her duties increase, he gets less and less of her attention.
After a while he may get only a few minutes of her time
because at the end of a hard day mothers are entitled to
some time free from any other demands. Since we seem
to need our husbands less, we can't understand why they
still need us the same.

We spend less and less intimate time with them until
seeds of rejection are planted and give way to bitterness,
shortness of temper and unkind words on their part.
These must be difficult times for any husband. But, they
must be understanding of mother's new role. And we
must be more careful not to close them out; for this could
be the beginning of the end. How sad that the very life
our love produces divides us.

Harold loved to spend as much time with our babies
as I did. He was always the one to get up at night in those
first few months to help get the children onto a schedule.
He would often lose as much sleep as I did. Fathers can

be very close to their children. They don't, however, seem to lose themselves in the children as we wives are known to do. Our husbands still need us — perhaps even more so. And when the children are grown and gone, we will have each other. We had better be steadily developing that relationship, or our husbands won't be there when we need them.

The Children Enter School

Another stage that we are ill prepared for is the entrance of the children into school. Life has been a whirlwind of activity for several years, and suddenly we find ourselves with extra time on our hands. This is when many mothers get hooked on the "soap operas" or on "romantic novels." This is amazing, since we have been longing for this valuable time. Instead of putting it to creative use, as the woman of Proverbs 31, we become bored and complacent and lose our self worth.

That free time during school hours could help us prepare for the full evenings. If we are not prepared, daddys will suffer once again. By the time we have prepared and served supper, done the dishes, given the children a bath, helped them with their homework, and gotten them safely into bed, fatigue takes over. When we hit the bed, we only have energy enough to pull the covers over our heads.

But, the lack of our husband's attention is not good for us either. His attention brings us much happiness. We need that intimate time together. Perhaps mothers in a similar situation should take a catnap in the afternoon and be ready to take time for the man they love.

Up, Up and Away

Parenthood is priceless, but, it is not forever. Children quickly grow into adolescents and adolescents into adults who take on their own lives. The time for parenting each child always seemed very short to us. Then, suddenly they were out on their own. Psychologists have developed a term for what happens to a mother when the children are all grown and gone from home (and she begins to wonder what her purpose in life is). They call it "the Empty Nest Syndrome." It is very real. It is another of those very serious periods of adjustment that can have its adverse effect on the marriage.

The early periods of parenthood demand that we hold our children close to give them warmth and security. But, very quickly we need to start releasing them to find their own way in the world. It doesn't happen overnight, but it does take place in rather large leaps that can be emotionally disconcerting.

The first day of elementary school is a "tear jerker." We think our heart will surely break. The more the children grow and learn and relate to other people outside the family, the closer they come to the day they leave us. They grow up, up, up and away.

During their adolescent years we begin to get the feeling they don't need us at all. It is not true, of course.

They need us very much during this critical period of development. Many mothers, however, are offended by their children's independence and begin to feel sorry for themselves. They often take out their frustrations on the children verbally. Father may suffer during this period of adjustment, as well. This is just another part of the growing process.

Mothers need to do some growing up of their own. They cannot expect the same level of affection from their children who are developing outside interests. Mother's reaction to this natural process can do irreparable damage to the relationship she cherishes with her children and with her husband.

The next big step children take in the growing process is graduating from high school and leaving for college or moving away from home. This can be a traumatic time for everyone concerned.

For years, even though the children have been growing up and needing us less and less — their lives filled with school activities and friends — at least they came home to eat and sleep. We were still a major part of their lives in that sense. Now, they must leave the nest and fly on their own. This is not a pleasant process for any parent.

We have very mixed feelings about seeing our little ones develop to this point: glad to see them doing so well, and sad to have to let go of them. Even though your heart aches, however, you know they must be free to fly. It hurts them too, but they need to stretch their wings and soar. There is so much living to do.

The Lord is gracious to help us in each of these major steps, for any of them can be emotionally upsetting and therefore detrimental to our wellbeing. We have closely allied ourselves emotionally with the children over a period of years, spending much time with them each day. Suddenly, they are gone, and we feel empty. We feel "taken for granted" and toy with the idea of "getting a real job" to prove our intellectual worth and our earning ability.

Those hours that we spent with the children must now be channeled into other creative activities. There are so many worthy things that can be accomplished for the family, for the community and for the church. We must grow with our children and not let any step in their development adversely affect our marital relationship.

God's Ideal

For so many years I considered the woman of Proverbs 31 to be an unobtainable ideal, God's super-woman. Yet He knows us, knows our worth, and knows our capabilities. He set those standards for womanhood Himself. They must, therefore, be obtainable. When we accomplish one thing, He has something else waiting for us to do. God created woman with a wonderful purpose in mind. She is not a lesser creature. Let us strive for God's best in our lives.

Through the years, when I meditated on God's woman of Proverbs 31, I thought to myself, "If a woman could do all that, why would she need a man?" I know now that it is because of the man in her life that the godly woman can do all those fantastic things. He is a respected man of the community, lending her a security and safety in which she can operate. He is the spiritual head over the household that she prides herself in protecting and providing for.

She has an incentive to manage her time well. She has a loving husband. Seeing his dedication and hard labor for the provision and welfare of the family, she cannot disappoint him by spoiling his hard work and dedication through her laziness. This virtuous wife is so dedicated to managing the affairs of the household that her husband can safely trust in her (Verse 11). What greater ambition could a woman have?

The Epilogue

Several things need to be said before we close this portion of the book:

1. Some of those who read the manuscript felt that Appendix A should be the first chapter of the book. It lays the biblical foundations for marriage. It is important, and I hope you will take time to read and study it. Because of its outline form, however, I am sure that many people would never pick up the book if I made it the first chapter. I hope the form we have chosen will satisfy both the casual reader and the serious student.

2. The book is bound to offend some people. After all, 50% of American marriages have already failed. My intention is not to offend those who have already failed, but to help rescue others from failure. Once a marriage has already failed, another situation entirely arises which is beyond the scope of this book — except in the case of those who are already remarried. I believe the principles outlined here will save second marriages and third marriages, as well.

3. We have not attempted to give specific solutions to specific situations, just general guidelines. Marital disputes can be so extremely complicated, with wrongs on both sides, that at times no living person can declare a solution. Although I don't profess to have all the answers, I know Someone who does. God ordained marriage. He knows what's wrong with yours and can remedy it, if you let Him. Commit your specific case to Him today, and EXPECT A MIRACLE!

EXPECT A MIRACLE!

Appendixes

Appendix A

Biblical Gems
Concerning Marriage

Scattered throughout the Bible we can find gems of wisdom that have their application in the marriage relationship. Here are a few of them for those who desire to delve deeper into the Bible teachings on this subject.

Job is one of the mysteries of Scripture. When did he live? We don't know. Nevertheless, we are blessed by his love of God, his determination to be faithful to God in his trials and the testimony of his ultimate restoration to prosperity. He showed great wisdom for a man of his wealth and stature:

> *I made a covenant with mine eyes; why then should I think upon a maid?*   Job 31:1

Abraham and Sarah derived great pleasure from their marriage. One of the things that made Sarah laugh when she heard the promise of the angel that she would have a child was the thought of having *"pleasure"* at her age:

> *Therefore Sarah laughed within herself, saying, After I am waxed old shall I have pleasure, my lord being old also?*   Genesis 18:12

Moses was used of God to deliver the Law, which we today find to be very harsh in respect to matters of marriage. Unfaithfulness to the marriage vows was regularly punished with the death penalty. The Law was God's way of showing man what was important to Him. It also had its tender side:

> *When a man hath taken a new wife, he shall not go out to war, neither shall he be charged with any business: but he shall be free at home one year, and shall cheer up his wife which he hath taken.*   Deuteronomy 24:5

We don't know much about Mrs. Moses. But, I'm sure she could tell us that Moses was a good husband. He didn't let the pressures of leading a couple million rebellious people through the wilderness keep him from being both a good father and husband. We should not be surprised to see the Scriptures record:

> *And Moses was an hundred and twenty years old when he died: his eye was not dim, nor his natural force abated.*   Deuteronomy 34:7

Joshua accepted the spiritual responsibility of husbands when he spoke for his entire family:

And if it seem evil unto you to serve the Lord, choose you this day whom ye will serve; whether the gods which your fathers served that were on the other side of the flood, or the gods of the Amorites, in whose land ye dwell: but as for me and my house, we will serve the Lord.   Joshua 24:15

David had his own marital tragedies. Saul took his first wife from him. When his enemies devastated his wilderness camp and carried captive his wife and children, he wept until there were no more tears. He erred badly in his affair with Bath-sheba and brought reproach upon all Israel. He knew God's promises for the home:

For the Lord God is a sun and shield: the Lord will give grace and glory: no good thing will he withhold from them that walk uprightly.   Psalms 84:11

There shall no evil befall thee, neither shall any plague come nigh thy dwelling.   Psalms 91:10

Hide not thy face from me in the day when I am in trouble; incline thine ear unto me: in the day when I call answer me speedily.   Psalms 102:2

But the mercy of the Lord is from everlasting to everlasting upon them that fear him, and his righteousness unto children's children;
Psalms 103:17

Thy wife [spouse] *shall be as a fruitful vine by the sides of thine house: thy children like olive plants round about thy table.*   Psalms 128:3

We have already mentioned <u>Solomon</u>'s tragedy. The important thing is that he learned from his mistakes and went on to teach others God's ways:

> *House and riches are the inheritance of fathers: and a*
> *prudent wife is from the Lord.*   Proverbs 19:14

> *And by knowledge shall the chambers be filled with all*
> *precious and pleasant riches.*   Proverbs 24:3

> *Lay not wait, O wicked man, against the dwelling of the*
> *righteous; spoil not his resting place:*
> Proverbs 24:15

> *When the wicked are multiplied, transgression increaseth:*
> *but the righteous shall see their fall.*
> Proverbs 29:16

Although Solomon considered life to be *"vanity,"* he knew that a proper marriage would bring great joy to this temporary existence we call "life":

> *Live joyfully with the wife whom thou lovest all the days of*
> *the life of thy vanity, which he hath given thee under the*
> *sun, all the days of thy vanity: for that is thy portion in this*
> *life, and in thy labour which thou takest under the sun.*
> Ecclesiastes 9:9

It was <u>Amos</u>, the Prophet, who asked that age-old question:

> *Can two walk together, except they be agreed?*
> Amos 3:3

Malachi, the last of the minor prophets, chided God's people for leaving that wonderful vision of the perfect marriage:

> *The Lord hath been witness between thee and the wife of thy youth, against whom thou hast dealt treacherously: yet is she thy companion, and the wife of thy covenant.*
>
> Malachi 2:14

The teachings of Jesus concerning marriage are widely quoted:

> *It hath been said, Whosoever shall put away his wife, let him give her a writing of divorcement: But I say unto you, That whosoever shall put away his wife, saving for the cause of fornication, causeth her to commit adultery: and whosoever shall marry her that is divorced committeth adultery.*   Matthew 5:31-32

> *Have ye not read, that he which made them at the beginning made them male and female, And said, For this cause shall a man leave father and mother, and shall cleave to his wife: and they twain shall be one flesh? Wherefore they are no more twain, but one flesh. What therefore God hath joined together, let not man put asunder.*
>
> *Moses because of the hardness of your hearts suffered you to put away your wives: but from the beginning it was not so. And I say unto you, Whosoever shall put away his wife, except it be for fornication, and shall marry another, committeth adultery: and whoso marrieth her which is put away doth commit adultery.*

His disciples say unto him, If the case of the man be so with his wife, it is not good to marry. But he said unto them, All men cannot receive this saying, save they to whom it is given. For there are some eunuchs, which were so born from their mother's womb: and there are some eunuchs, which were made eunuchs of men: and there be eunuchs, which have made themselves eunuchs for the kingdom of heaven's sake. He that is able to receive it, let him receive it.   Matthew 19:4-6, 8-9 & 10-12

For the hardness of your heart he [Moses] *wrote you this precept* [law of divorce]. *But from the beginning of the creation God made them male and female. For this cause shall a man leave his father and mother, and cleave to his wife; And they twain shall be one flesh: so then they are no more twain, but one flesh. What therefore God hath joined together, let not man put asunder.*
And he saith unto them, Whosoever shall put away his wife, and marry another, committeth adultery against her. And if a woman shall put away her husband, and be married to another, she committeth adultery.
                          Mark 10:5-9 & 11-12

Whosoever putteth away his wife, and marrieth another, committeth adultery: and whosoever marrieth her that is put away from her husband committeth adultery.
                          Luke 16:18

Jesus attended a wedding in Cana of Galilee with both His family and disciples and chose the wedding feast as the place to perform His first public miracle, a provision for the feast (John 2:1-11). He thus put His seal of approval upon marriage. We will be joined to Him in a far more intimate way in the future, He being the Heavenly Bridegroom and we the Bride for a wedding in heaven. There God will express His love to us in *"the marriage of the Lamb"* (Revelation 19:7).

Paul covered many aspects of marriage in one section of his first letter to the Corinthians:

> *Now concerning the things whereof ye wrote unto me: It is good for a man not to touch a woman. Nevertheless, to avoid fornication, let every man have his own wife, and let every woman have her own husband. Let the husband render unto the wife due benevolence: and likewise also the wife unto the husband. The wife hath not power of her own body, but the husband: and likewise also the husband hath not power of his own body, but the wife. Defraud ye not one the other, except it be with consent for a time, that ye may give yourselves to fasting and prayer; and come together again, that Satan tempt you not for your incontinency. But I speak this by permission, and not of commandment. For I would that all men were even as I myself. But every man hath his proper gift of God, one after this manner, and another after that. I say therefore to the unmarried and widows, It is good for them if they abide even as I. But if they cannot contain, let them marry: for it is better to marry than to burn. And unto the married I command, yet not I, but the Lord, Let not the wife depart from her husband: But and if she depart, let her remain unmarried, or be reconciled to her husband: and let not the husband put away his wife.*
> *But to the rest speak I, not the Lord: If any brother hath a wife that believeth not, and she be pleased to dwell with*

him, let him not put her away. And the woman which hath an husband that believeth not, and if he be pleased to dwell with her, let her not leave him. For the unbelieving husband is sanctified by the wife, and the unbelieving wife is sanctified by the husband: else were your children unclean; but now are they holy. But if the unbelieving depart, let him depart. A brother or a sister is not under bondage in such cases: but God hath called us to peace. For what knowest thou, O wife, whether thou shalt save thy husband? or how knowest thou, O man, whether thou shalt save thy wife?

But as God hath distributed to every man, as the Lord hath called every one, so let him walk. And so ordain I in all churches. Is any man called being circumcised? let him not become uncircumcised. Is any called in uncircumcision? let him not be circumcised. Circumcision is nothing, and uncircumcision is nothing, but the keeping of the commandments of God. Let every man abide in the same calling wherein he was called. Art thou called being a servant? care not for it: but if thou mayest be made free, use it rather. For he that is called in the Lord, being a servant, is the Lord's freeman: likewise also he that is called, being free, is Christ's servant. Ye are bought with a price; be not ye the servants of men. Brethren, let every man, wherein he is called, therein abide with God.

Now concerning virgins I have no commandment of the Lord: yet I give my judgment, as one that hath obtained mercy of the Lord to be faithful. I suppose therefore that this is good for the present distress, I say, that it is good for a man so to be. Art thou bound unto a wife? seek not to be loosed. Art thou loosed from a wife? seek not a wife. But and if thou marry, thou hast not sinned; and if a virgin marry, she hath not sinned. Nevertheless such shall have *trouble in the flesh: but I spare you. But this I say, brethren, the time is short: it remaineth, that both they that have wives be as though they had none; And they that weep, as though they wept not; and they that rejoice, as though they rejoiced not; and they that buy, as though they possessed not; And they that use this world, as not abusing it: for the fashion of this world passeth away.*

But I would have you without carefulness. He that is unmarried careth for the things that belong to the Lord, how he may please the Lord: But he that is married careth for the things that are of the world, how he may please his wife. There is difference also between a wife and a virgin. The unmarried woman careth for the things of the Lord, that she may be holy both in body and in spirit: but she that is married careth for the things of the world, how she may please her husband. And this I speak for your own profit; not that I may cast a snare upon you, but for that which is comely, and that ye may attend upon the Lord without distraction.

But if any man think that he behaveth himself uncomely toward his virgin, if she pass the flower of her age, and need so require, let him do what he will, he sinneth not: let them marry. Nevertheless he that standeth stedfast in his heart, having no necessity, but hath power over his own will, and hath so decreed in his heart that he will keep his virgin, doeth well. So then he that giveth her in marriage doeth well; but he that giveth her not in marriage doeth better.

The wife is bound by the law as long as her husband liveth;

*but if her husband be dead, she is at liberty to be married
to whom she will; only in the Lord. But she is happier if she
so abide, after my judgment: and I think also that I have
the Spirit of God.*   1 Corinthians 7:1-40*

If every Christian young person would study this chapter
over and over before making a decision about their future,
we would have a fraction of the present divorce rate. Paul
further taught:

*Let love be without dissimulation. Abhor that which is evil;
cleave to that which is good.*   Romans 12:9

*Love worketh no ill to his neighbour: therefore love is the
fulfilling of the law.*   Romans 13:10

*Charity suffereth long, and is kind; charity envieth not;
charity vaunteth not itself, is not puffed up, doth not
behave itself unseemly, seeketh not her own, is not easily
provoked, thinketh no evil; rejoiceth not in iniquity, but
rejoiceth in the truth; beareth all things, believeth all
things, hopeth all things, endureth all things. Charity
never faileth.*   1 Corinthians 13:4-8

*Wives, submit yourselves unto your own husbands, as
unto the Lord. For the husband is the head of the wife, even
as Christ is the head of the church: and he is the saviour
of the body. Therefore as the church is subject unto Christ,
so let the wives be to their own husbands in every thing.
Husbands, love your wives, even as Christ also loved the
church, and gave himself for it; That he might sanctify
and cleanse it with the washing of water by the word, That
he might present it to himself a glorious church, not having*

spot, or wrinkle, or any such thing; but that it should be holy and without blemish. So ought men to love their wives as their own bodies. He that loveth his wife loveth himself. For no man ever yet hated his own flesh; but nourisheth and cherisheth it, even as the Lord the church: For we are members of his body, of his flesh, and of his bones. For this cause shall a man leave his father and mother, and shall be joined unto his wife, and they two shall be one flesh. This is a great mystery: but I speak concerning Christ and the church. Nevertheless let every one of you in particular so love his wife even as himself; and the wife see that she reverence her husband. Ephesians 5:22-33

A bishop then must be blameless, the husband of one wife, vigilant, sober, of good behaviour, given to hospitality, apt to teach; 1 Timothy 3:2

But if any provide not for his own, and specially for those of his own house, he hath denied the faith, and is worse than an infidel. 1 Timothy 5:8

But godliness with contentment is great gain. For we brought nothing into this world, and it is certain we can carry nothing out. And having food and raiment let us be therewith content. But they that will be rich fall into temptation and a snare, and into many foolish and hurtful lusts, which drown men in destruction and perdition. For the love of money is the root of all evil: which while some coveted after, they have erred from the faith, and pierced themselves through with many sorrows. But thou, O man of God, flee these things; and follow after righteousness, godliness, faith, love, patience, meekness. 1 Timothy 6:6-11

In a greater sense, every verse of the Bible applies to marriage. For if you can't live the Bible at home, where can you live it? *"Pure religion"* is not defined by public displays of our faith, but in the daily living of it.

> *Pure religion and undefiled before God and the Father is this, To visit the fatherless and widows in their affliction, and to keep himself unspotted from the world.*
> James 1:27

Appendix B

Index of Bible References

The Old Testament

The New Testament

Verse	*Page*
Matthew 5:20	85
Matthew 5:23-24	32
Matthew 5:31-32	109
Matthew 5:41	61
Matthew 6:12-15	33
Matthew 18:6	32
Matthew 19:4-6	9, 109
Matthew 19:8-9	109
Matthew 19:10-12	109
Matthew 22:30	75
Matthew 23:1-7	48
Matthew 25:40	35
Mark 10:5-9	110
Mark 10:9	77
Mark 10:11-12	110
Mark 10:42-44	49
Mark 10:45	49
Mark 12:25	75
Mark 12:41-44	64
Luke 16:18	110
Luke 23:34	30
John 2:1-11	110
Romans 7:2	77
Romans 8:7	38
Romans 12:9	114
Romans 12:10	45
Romans 13:10	114
Romans 14:13	47
Romans 15:7	45
1 Corinthians 5:9	85
1 Corinthians 5:11	85
1 Corinthians 6:15	85
1 Corinthians 7:1-40	111-114